CRUSOE

And His Consequences

JAMES DUNKERLEY

OR Books

New York · London

© 2019 James Dunkerley

All rights information: rights@orbooks.com
Visit our website at www.orbooks.com

First printing 2019

Library of Congress Cataloging-in-Publication Data: A catalog record for this book is available from the Library of Congress.
British Library Cataloging in Publication Data: A catalog record for this book is available from the British Library.

Typeset by Lapiz Digital. Printed by BookMobile, USA, and CPI, UK.

paperback ISBN 978-1-68219-202-3 • ebook ISBN 978-1-68219-205-4

CRUSOE

And His Consequences

To Arianna
and to the memory of Uta

CONTENTS

Preface   1

Robinson Crusoe   17

Daniel Defoe   143

Acknowledgments   245

Notes   249

Everything happens as though, on this fictional island, Robinson Crusoe were reinventing sovereignty, technology, tools, the machine, the becoming-machine of the tool, and prayers, God, true religion.

—*Jacques Derrida*

Robinson Crusoe is one of the great myths of modern civilization; the story celebrates Western Civilization's material triumphs and the strength of its rational will to conquer the environment; and it also prefigures the spiritual loneliness and social alienation which have accompanied its progress.

—*Ian Watt*

Defoe is a risk-taker, an opportunist, a hired pen, a showman, an at-times dubious businessman who cheated his mother-in-law and believed in the slave trade, but he is *au fond* the journalist as civic hero, the master polemicist of his age.

—*Tom Paulin*

However, it is certain, that the Sale of a Book chiefly depends on the Universality of the Subject, and that the most excellent do not meet with the greatest Success; and accordingly, we find, that *Robinson Crusoe* sells quicker than *Locke* on Human Understanding . . . is it not sufficiently known, that some have acquired Estates, by printing Tom Thumb, Riddles, Songs, Fables, the Pilgrim's Progress and such like common Trumpery?

—*A Letter to the Society of Booksellers*

Whatever else he was, he was never that [a gentleman]. He was by turns a tradesman, an adventurer, a radical pamphleteer and agitator, a reporter, a spy, a gallant crusader, a crawling sycophant, a man accepted in court circles and once the confidant of the King and then able to plunge with equal zest into the lowest life of London; for months or even years on end, his diligent biographers cannot track him down through those murky, labyrinthine lairs. Half his life he seemed to be bombarding Ministers with far-seeing schemes for new trading projects, for founding new colonies, for military expeditions, for old-age pensions and maritime insurance, for establishing academies for education to asylums for the insane. Through the other half he was getting practical experience with 'that worst of devils, poverty'.

—*Michael Foot*

PREFACE

The onset of every year proffers mixed lessons from the past and promises for the time up ahead. The year 1719 was no different from any other in this regard, whether we open it, in Gregorian style, on 1 January or on 23 March, according to the Julian calendar which prevailed in the young United Kingdom of Great Britain in 1719 and would not be replaced until 1751.

Of course, lessons and promises seldom allow for surprises, and when the Bank of England rate was set at 5 per cent in April 1719, nobody knew that it would endure as a base rate for over a century. Equally, when Robert Walpole sought to fix the interest on the surging national debt at that selfsame rate, he could pretty much rely upon the support of Daniel Defoe, whose *Fair Payment, No Spunge* argued that the debt could thereby be cleared in twenty-two years and without the highly risky speculation to which it was subject in the slippery directorial hands of the South Sea Company. Walpole and Defoe did not get their way, and the following year the Company's 'bubble' burst in spectacular fashion—the first real market failure of the modern financial era.

There were better prospects for trading in the greater Caribbean and northern seas when news reached London of the death in the Carolinas of the pirate Blackbeard (Edward Teach) in November 1718. Blackbeard, who was based in the Bahamian island of New Providence, had taken to blockading the then unprotected settlement of Charles Town (present-day Charleston, South Carolina) and ransoming its inhabitants. A fortnight later his associate Stede Bonnet, the 'Gentleman Pirate' from Barbados, was hanged in Charles Town, having reneged on an earlier promise to abjure the life of a refined corsair in exchange for the king's pardon. It would, though, be two more years before 'Calico Jack' Rackham, whose ships first flew the 'Jolly Roger' and who had likewise received a pardon only to return to piracy, was strung up in Port Royal, Jamaica. The image of Blackbeard's braided and beribboned beard has endured through the Hollywood *Pirates of the Caribbean* franchise, the comedic voicing of which—let alone the Rolling Stones mimicry—would have wholly bemused the nervous settlers, merchants, and administrators of the first British Empire. For a good sense of what they confronted, have a look at Daniel Defoe's *A General History of the Pyrates* (1724).

In 1719 Defoe was firmly based in London, but he had spent much time in Scotland and continued to keep a close eye on that country, where the effort to restore to the throne the 'Old Pretender', James Stuart, had collapsed but not disappeared after the failed uprising of 1715. The next year Britain reached a peace settlement with France, but she was now at war again with Spain, which took up the Jacobite cause in supporting a chaotic invasion of western Scotland in April 1719, when Spanish regulars were joined by warriors from the Mackenzie and Cameron clans. These forces were routed at the Battle of Glen Shiel, near Inverness, on 9 June 1719

PREFACE

by General Wightman with a thousand men and four Coehorn mortars, introduced to the country by the Dutch, whose Protestant lineage had been installed in 1688 precisely to replace the Stuart line. Most famous amongst the defeated insurrectionaries on that day was Rob Roy Macgregor. Rob Roy rustled cattle, and so was no less an outlaw than the Caribbean pirates, but he survived the charred battlefield as well as eviction and the destruction of his estate, receiving a royal pardon in 1727. Buoyed up by Walter Scott's Waverley novel, the resurgence of Scottish nationalism in the late twentieth century, and Liam Neeson's muscular depiction in the eponymous film of 1995, his name is at least recognised today.

No blockbuster could so readily be constructed from Eliza Haywood's romantic novel of 1719, *Love in Excess*, in which high passion, misunderstood letters, and a peculiarly feminist mix of castaway negligées and total-truth-telling yielded a happy finale for those principals fortunate enough not to run onto swords and still living as 'great and loving examples of conjugal affection'. With Aphra Behn and Delarivier Manley, who wrote before her, Haywood belonged to 'the fair triumvirate of wit', but their adventure and contemporary popularity—Defoe knew full well what he was up against—has not been fully respected by posterity.

Conjugal affection is conspicuous by its absence from the greatest literary legacy we have received from that year—the novel now known simply as *Robinson Crusoe*, published by the hyper-active Defoe in London two weeks after the Spanish had landed at Lochalsh. Of course, *Robinson Crusoe* has appeared in movies and on TV in myriad forms, but no major film has ever come close to capturing its essence. This text, none the less, became

3

one of the most influential in and beyond the Western World over the next three hundred years, exercising a profound impact not just on literature but also on how succeeding generations debated the nature of individual solitude, work, colonial and racial relations, economics, dreams, 'providence', and human relations with the rest of the animal world.

*

It's just possible that you have already read the full, unabridged text of Daniel Defoe's *The Life and Strange Surprizing Adventures of Robinson Crusoe*, published on 25 April 1719. You might, however, be awaiting an experience like that of the great historian Christopher Hill:

> Those who, like myself, first encountered *Robinson Crusoe* in an abridged edition are surprised when they read the original. It seems a very long time before we get to the point. An account of the hero's early life occupies the first 50 or so pages, one-seventh of Part I, before he is shipwrecked on his island. The original, moreover, looks much more like a protestant homily or moral fable—a 'parable' as the Preface to Part II describes it—than the abridgements which made it such a popular children's story.[1]

Yet, if '. . . almost everybody who picks up *Robinson Crusoe* can outline some of its episodes before he starts reading', that applies only to what Hill calls Part I.[2] It is very unlikely indeed that you have read Part II, *The Farther Adventures of Robinson Crusoe,* published on 20 August 1719; and, unless you are a dedicated Defoe scholar or greatly attracted to the intellectual history

PREFACE

of the paranormal, it is ardently to be hoped that you have not sought literary reward in Part III, *Serious Reflections during the Life and Surprising Adventures of Robinson Crusoe: with his Vision of the Angelick World,* published on 6 August 1720. This last volume was something of a *post hoc facto* explication of Crusoe's—never Defoe's—composition of the previous volumes. Even more rambling than them, and with absolutely minimal pretence at providing adventure-added, it soon disappeared into an afterlife of consolidated editions. Part II was also less popular than its predecessor but throughout much of the eighteenth century continued to be bound together with it.

Part I, of course, is wholly different, even if it was not until the 1750s that it was once again being published on its own. Four official editions were issued—at the price of five shillings, equivalent to two days' pay of a skilled urban worker—in the weeks of mid-1719 up to the appearance of Part II, by which time Crusoe/Defoe was already fulminating against the energetic competition of pirate versions. The narrative—the term 'novel' was rarely used by Defoe and was not common before the mid-nineteenth century—was serialised over seventy-eight instalments in the *Original London Post, or Heathcot's Intelligence* between October 1719 and March 1720.[3]

Such early success barely slowed down, either at home or abroad. By 1900 there were at least two hundred English editions, filling sixteen columns of the catalogue of the British Museum. Translations began within weeks, with fourteen into French between 1720 and 1729, nine into German between 1720 and 1783, five into Dutch and five into Italian up to 1791. Perhaps unsurprisingly, the 'rugged individualism' that will be discussed shortly, attracted Benjamin Franklin, who was in London in the 1720s and who lauded the book in his *Autobiography*, forming part of a distinct republican enthusiasm that yielded over a hundred editions between 1774 and 1830.[4] Thereafter only the most zealous bibliophile can keep up with translations, and, with versions in Maltese, Coptic, and Estonian as well as Welsh, Hebrew, and Maori, the best approach might be to seek out which language groups still lack their own version of *Crusoe*. It is, though, worth noting that before 1836 there was no translation in Spain, where the Inquisition—not overlooked in the original— was at work well into the nineteenth century.[5]

If the present book has an 'argument' in the sense employed by social scientists and lawyers, it is that Ian Watt was correct, and that *Crusoe* constitutes a core mythic text of Western and capitalist civilisation over the last three centuries. In the words of Robert MacDonald,

> We know that the book is full of faults, that it is repetitious and often boring, that it is sloppily written by a forgetful author. We are aware that the time scheme is improbable and the end of the novel tacked on . . . We know too that all these things matter very little, since the book has a mythic simplicity, an appeal that owes little to realism and nothing to chronology.[6]

In MacDonald's case, Defoe eventually provides, from the Godhead to the psyche, a comprehensive portrait of 'order'. Watt takes a rather different line, admiring the text's 'realism' at several levels.

Arguments of this type could, of course, be both verified and falsified, but I am not going there in the pages that follow. This is not a specialist book written by an expert. There are some endnotes, but they are there to keep

THE

LIFE

AND

STRANGE SURPRIZING

ADVENTURES

OF

ROBINSON CRUSOE,

Of *TORK,* Mariner:

Who lived Eight and Twenty Years,
all alone in an un-inhabited Island on the
Coast of America, near the Mouth of
the Great River of Oroonoque;

Having been cast on Shore by Shipwreck, wherein all the Men perished but himself.

WITH

An Account how he was at last as strangely deliver'd by PYRATES.

Written by Himself.

LONDON:
Printed for W. Taylor at the *Ship* in *Pater-Noster-
Row.* MDCCXIX.

The frontispiece and title page of the first edition of *Robinson Crusoe.*

the experts off as much of my case as I can contrive. This is a book written by an engrossed and enthusiastic beginner who, following Hill's experience, has wanted to discover why a narrative text that is in so many ways a dreadful mess has come to be 'a classic', not just in literary terms but in those of economics ('political arithmetick'), politics, and popular culture as well. On the assumption that even if you have read the full original text, a little refreshment of its outer lineaments and style might help, I have sought to provide a synopsis of the story in the following pages here. This is, of course, my 'take' on the book, and I am not an accomplished editor—not least in choosing between the sundry inconsistencies, particularly in terms of timing, in the story.[7] It really would be best if you first read or re-read the original as a whole. If in more than momentary doubt about that, please stop, and go do it now.[8]

For Coleridge, whose admiration for the book has rarely been outstripped, 'our imagination is kept in full play, excited to the highest, yet all the while we are touching or touched by a common flesh and blood'.[9] Perhaps it is no surprise that he thought it a 'happy nightmare'? From Peter Hulme's post-colonial and Caribbean perspective, '[the] island episode of *Robinson Crusoe* is mythic in the same way as *The Tempest*: it provides a simplifying crucible in which complexities can be reduced to their essential components'.[10] That may well be the reason why *Crusoe* has seldom been dislodged from its role as exemplar for economic theories—either directly or through its multiple derivations, exploited especially by neo-classical marginalists from the nineteenth century onwards. As a consequence Karl Marx, who initially viewed the novel as anticipating social alienation, came to criticise the likes of Smith and Ricardo for abusing 'Robinsonades' in the cause of explicating capitalist 'logic'. In 2018 my granddaughter, during her first year as a geography and economics university student, was given *Crusoe* as an illustration of both British colonialism and—rather more ambitiously—relative prices. As we will see from the studies of Matthew Watson, the idealisation of *Crusoe* has become a veritable fixture in the textbooks and syllabi of mainstream economics.

Of course, a multitude of inaccuracies and misconceptions can proliferate in the brightness of myth. The disciples of 'rational actor' economics may well be singularly unable to see the wood for the trees, but the best of the rest of us can readily trip up in our confidence about the story. Marx himself erroneously depicts Crusoe retrieving a watch from the shipwreck, whilst Toni Morrison confuses the nationality of the mutineers and mislocates Friday's father in the flow of the story.[11] This, though, is not really the fault of Defoe, who

> obeys more fully than ever before the purpose of language as Locke redefined it: 'to convey knowledge of things'. Defoe concentrates his description on the primary qualities of objects as Locke saw them: especially solidity, extension and number; and he gives them in the simplest language.[12]

Rather, as suggested by James Sutherland, one of Defoe's best biographers, forgetfulness is at the very heart of the myth:

> To read *Robinson Crusoe* is to be compelled to face up to all sorts of physical problems that civilized man has long since forgotten. It

is in some sense to retrace the history of the human race; it is certainly to look again with the unspoilt eyes of childhood on many things that one had long since ceased to notice at all.[13]

In the face of such comprehensive attainment, it is pretty hard to avoid going beyond the words to their author—Defoe's name did finally appear in that guise on an edition of 1781—even if he was 'a writer as complex and as contradictory as any we can read in English literature . . . there are many Defoes'.[14] The second part of the present book is therefore biographical in approach, and, like the first, entirely reliant on the scholarship of experts.

Even with a quite formidable record of archival research and documentary detective work over three hundred years, it is exceptionally difficult to keep this individual in sight; and that applies just as much to those who say that there is no Defoe to be known beyond his writings simply because there is still no settled agreement on what Defoe did or did not write. His name appears on just four of the 247 items allowed in 1994 by Messrs. Furbank and Owens as stylistically and circumstantially to be by Daniel Defoe.[15] Luckily, *Crusoe* is among the recognised canon, alongside *An Essay Upon Projects, The True-Born Englishman, Jure Divino, The Family Instructor, Moll Flanders, Roxana, The Storm, The Journal of a Plague Year, A Tour through the Whole Island of Great Britain, The Compleat English Tradesman, The Political History of the Devil, Conjugal Lewdness* and others, besides the roughly four million words of the *Review* published up to three times a week between 1704 and 1713. There are words enough in quantity, then, but, just as they vary in quality, so too do they often clash in sense and message.

PREFACE

As with the book, so with the author—writers on economics and politics find in Defoe much more than a simple solitary trajectory. For Jurgen Habermas, writing in the sterile climate of late 1950s West Germany under the *Marxisant* influence of the Frankfurt School, Defoe plays a walk-on part in an emergent 'bourgeois public sphere' between feudalism and the still unevolved capitalist civil society associated with the industrial revolution. The principal vehicles for this contested public space are the coffeehouse and newspaper. Similar to the case of Michel Foucault, who was developing for a rather later period the thesis of a transition from exemplary corporal and capital punishment to the regime of the panopticon and internalised social discipline, Habermas's thesis has been subject to a veritable barrage of historiographical and analytical objections.[16] And, as with Foucault, that has not dented its influence a great deal. We shall see that Defoe not only 'wrote for bread' but also out of conviction; as a result, he was jailed several times. More than occasionally the victim of judicial and vigilante violence, he ensured that the Stoke Newington mansion bought in 1708 on a curve of business success was liberally supplied with bolt-holes and escape-hatches. There were distinct limits to the 'public sphere', and even into his forties Defoe was a complete champion at testing them out.

Defoe died in the City of London hiding from his creditors. Both his private and public lives may properly be associated with 'capitalism' in so far as it relates to the 'financial revolution' from the 1690s, rather than the emergence of manufacturing industry a century later. This is why J.G.A. Pocock allocates him a prominent role in *The Machiavellian Moment*, during which, in a kind of echo of the Habermas and Foucault theses, the locus of public virtue shifts from military prowess associated with the responsibilities of feudal hierarchy to the upkeep of government by the funding of public debt, parallel to the replacement of Stuart absolutism by parliamentary majoritarianism as the power that sourced Britain's army and navy.[17]

Here again, no clear picture can be agreed upon. Defoe was unarguably a fervent opponent of Restoration power, particularly with regard to its punitive religious restrictions. Equally, he was an admirer and energetic supporter of William of Orange, whose wars on continental Europe obeyed the strategic interests of the Dutch—who had fought two wars against England in living memory—and were politically divisive at home. Yet after William's death in 1702, Defoe, who seems to have introduced the term 'balance of power', was an energetic proponent of a 'realist' approach to foreign policy, as illustrated by a cool editorial of April 1709 in the *Review*:

> We do not fight against France as a Kingdom, or against the King of France as a King, no nor as a Tyrant insulting the Liberties of his own subjects; but we fight against France as a kingdom grown too great for her neighbours, and against the King of France as an invader of other nation's rights . . . we fight to reduce him to a condition that he may be no more dangerous to his neighbours.[18]

There are moments—as with the Palatine Crisis of the same year—when Defoe's dissenting Protestant loyalties threatened to overwhelm the sobriety of his international analysis, and the South Sea Bubble coming on the lee of *Crusoe* took the wind out of his favourite overseas scheme to colonise Patagonia. However, the process of personal ageing, the decompression of European politics after the Peace of Utrecht in 1713, and the failure of the Jacobite uprising of 1715 made Defoe's general trajectory unsurprising—away from popular sovereignty, through court Whiggism, and into the service of moderate Toryism. Small wonder, then, that this political shape-shifter attracted bilious invective, such as that contained in *Judas Discuver'd* of 1713:

> Of all the Writers that have prostituted their Pens, either to encourage *Faction*, oblige a party, or for their own *Mercenary Ends*; the *Person* here mentioned is the Vilest. An *Animal* who shifts his Shape oftner than *Proteus*, and goes backwards and forwards like a Hunted hare; a thorough-pac'd, true-bred *Hypocrite*, an *High-Church Man* one Day, and a *Rank Whig* the next; Like the *Satyr* in the *Fable*, he blows Hot and Cold with the same breath, and is in reality a downright *Fanatick*.[19]

Two years later, Defoe took the quite remarkable step for him of casting aside anonymity in *An Appeal to the Honour and Justice Though It Be of His Worst Enemies* to defend his conduct, based upon

> Duty . . . to go along with every Ministry, so far as they did not break in upon the Constitution, and the laws and Liberties of my Country; my Part being only the Duty of a Subject, (*viz*) to submit to all lawful Commands.[20]

On one matter, however, whatever his personal fortunes, Daniel Defoe remained constant throughout his adult life—the promotion of national and overseas trade. An early passage in his first substantial publication, *An Essay Upon Projects*, published in 1697 but probably written five years earlier, has a resonance of the advocates of globalisation in the 1990s:

> Ships are sent from Port to Port, as Markets and Merchandizes differ, by the help of strange and Universal Intelligence; wherein some are so exquisite, so swift, and so exact, that a Merchant sitting at home in his Counting-house, at once converses with all Parts of the known World. This, and Travel, makes a True-bred Merchant the most Intelligent Man in the World.

That short book ends with the matter of words. So, as a first step in adjusting to the cadences that the English language took three hundred years back, it seems right to finish these opening remarks with a quotation of those that close *An Essay Upon Projects*:

> As for such who read books only to find out the author's faux pas, who will quarrel at the meanness of style, errors of pointing, dullness of expression, or the like, I have but little to say to them. I thought I had corrected it very carefully, and yet some mis-pointings and small errors have slipped me, which it is too late to help. As to language, I have been rather careful to make it speak English suitable to the manner of the story than to dress it up with exactness of style, choosing rather to have it free and familiar, according to the nature of essays, than to strain at perfection of language which I rather wish for than pretend to be master of.[21]

PREFACE

Note: Where I have quoted Defoe directly from an original edition I have retained his style. Where I have used a secondary source for quotation I have followed the style of that source. According to the Bank of England's calculation of average inflation, goods and services worth £1 in 1700 were valued at £195 in 2017.

ROBINSON CRUSOE

The Story—Outline and Excerpts

> I was born in the year 1632, in the city of *York*, of a good family, tho' not of that country, my father being a foreigner of *Bremen*, who settled first at *Hull*: He got a good estate by merchandise, and leaving off his trade, lived afterward at *York*, from whence he married my mother, whose relations were named *Robinson*, a very good family in that country, and from whom I was called *Robinson Kreutznaer;* but by the usual corruption of words in *England*, we are now called, nay we call our selves, and write our name *Crusoe,* and so my companions always call'd me. (5)

Crusoe's father sought to impress upon his son the importance of 'the middle station . . . which was not expos'd to so many vicissitudes as the higher or lower part of humankind' (6), and that, accordingly, he should settle down to a safe career, rather than indulge his desire to go to sea. However, aged nineteen, he did just that, from Hull, boarding a ship to London, without asking parental permission.

The ship was very soon struck by a fierce storm, and Crusoe, 'inexpressibly sick in body and terrify'd in my mind . . . was overtaken by the judgement of Heaven for my wicked leaving of my father's house, and abandoning my duty' (7). Moreover, after the storm abated and another six days' sailing, the ship was hit by a second storm, which tore the craft apart and forced the crew to abandon her in boats within sight of the shore near Yarmouth. But Crusoe, instead of returning to Yorkshire, goes to London, and falls in with the master of a ship working the coast of Guinea (Africa). On his first voyage, he sets out with £40 raised from relations and returns with £300 worth of gold. Obviously encouraged to repeat the experience, he sets out again, but the ship is attacked by a Turkish pirate working out of Sallee (Morocco), with Crusoe taken prisoner and held personally by the pirate captain.

There he stays, with 'no fellow-slave, no *Englishman, Irishman,* or *Scotsman* there but myself; so that for two years, tho' I often pleased myself with the imagination, yet I never had the least encouraging prospect of putting it into practice' (18). Having encouraged his 'patron' to let him go fishing for him in the company of one of the captain's kinsmen and a youth, Crusoe develops a plan to escape, persuading the 'Moor' to let him supply the boat for a long outing. At sea, he throws overboard his captor, who, threatened with his own gun, swims for shore.

> When he was gone I turn'd to the boy, who they call'd *Xury,* and said to him, *Xury,* if you will be faithful to me I'll make you a great man, but if you will not stroak your face to be true to me, *that is, swear by* Mahomet *and his father's beard*, I must throw you into the

sea too; the boy smil'd in my face, and spoke so innocently that I could not mistrust him . . . (20–21)

The pair head south, where Crusoe reckons they need to travel some hundred and fifty miles along the 'Barbarian Coast' to escape the reach of the Emperor of Morocco. They see great creatures on the shore and hear 'horrible noises, and hideous cries and howlings' (22). On one landing for fresh water Xury shoots a lion, which provides no food but, after much effort, is skinned for its hide. They see people, 'quite black and stark naked', on the beaches but Xury persuades Crusoe not to approach them, but when he shoots an attacking leopard which approaches the boat in menacing fashion, the *Negroes* give them food and water, which last them for another eleven days until they are able to attract the attention of a Portuguese ship. The friendly captain offers to carry them to safety, guarantee Crusoe's possessions, and buy the boat for a proposed eighty pieces of eight, proposing to buy Xury for a further sixty, which Crusoe resists until the captain assures him that 'he would give the boy an obligation to set him free in ten years, if he turn'd Christian; upon this, and *Xury* saying he was willing to go to him, I let the Captain have him' (29).

With money for the boat and the hides of the lion and tiger as well as Xury, Crusoe, who regrets the last sale, is able to travel to Brazil, buy land, and establish a plantation. The Portuguese captain takes back to Europe Crusoe's letters, some money for the widow of a British ship that was wrecked, and news of his adventures for London merchants through whom he hoped to trade.

> Neither was this all; but my goods being all *English* manufactures, such as cloth, stuffs, bays, and things particularly valuable and desirable in the country, I found means to sell them to a very great advantage; so that Might say, I had more than four times the value of my first cargo, and was now infinitely beyond my poor neighbour, I mean in the advancement of my plantation; for the first thing I did, I bought me a *Negro* slave . . . (31)

But Crusoe's very success—fifty rolls of tobacco at a hundredweight shipped to Lisbon—raised his ambitions further, so that after four years' prosperity he was again unable to cleave to his father's advice for the securities of 'the middle station'. He agreed with his fellow planters that he would oversee a voyage to Guinea to buy Negroes to be sold privately back in Brazil. The ship, of one hundred twenty tons, six guns, and fourteen crew, left Brazil eight years to the day after Crusoe had deserted his parents 'and obey'd blindly the dictates of my fancy rather than my reason' (34). Starting out in good weather, the ship was at 7 degrees 22 minutes North when it was struck by a hurricane, being driven out of control for a full twelve days, with the loss of two men and a boy. During a break in the storm the Master reckoned they were 11 degrees North, somewhere between the Amazon and Orinoco rivers, so they decided to make for Barbados. But they were soon hit by a second storm, so severe that the remaining crew sought to row to a nearby shore since no sail could be made and the ship was breaking up. Having launched the boat, however,

> A raging wave, mountain-like, came rowling a-stern of us, and plainly bad us expect the *coup de grace* . . . it took us with such fury, that it overset the boat at once . . . Nothing can describe the confusion of thought which I felt when I sunk into the water; for tho' I swam very well, yet I could not deliver my self from the waves so as to draw breath, till that wave having driven me . . . and having spent itself, went back, and left me upon the land almost dry, but half-dead with the water I took in . . . The wave that came upon me again, buried me at once 20 or 30 foot deep in its own body; and I could feel myself carried away with a mighty force and swiftness . . . (37)

Crusoe is twice more swept up by huge waves, dashed, nearly senseless, against rocks, until he is able to struggle to a rock and wait for the sea to abate a little and get to land.

> I . . . began to look up and thank God that my life was sav'd in a case wherein there was some minutes before scarce any room to hope. I believe it is impossible to express to the life what the extasies and transports of the soul are, when it is so sav'd, as I may say, out of the very grave . . . I walk'd about on the shore, lifting up my hands, and my whole being, as I may say, wrapt up in the contemplation of my deliverance, making a thousand gestures and motions which I cannot describe, reflecting on all my comrades that were drown'd, and that there should not be one soul sav'd but

my self; for, as for them, I never saw them afterwards, or any sign of them, except three of their hats, one cap, and two shoes that were not fellows. (38–39)

Crusoe has nothing but the drenched clothes he is wearing, a knife, a pipe, and a little tobacco. He expects to die of hunger or be consumed by wild beasts. With no hopeful prospect, he finds a tree, in the branches of which he sleeps the first night in what would become his island. It is 30 September 1659.

*

Crusoe descends from his 'apartment in the tree' the next morning to a calm sea, with the shipwreck two miles off and a quarter of a mile off-shore at ebb tide. There now begins a two-week series of trips to the ship to remove everything of use that he can find. The first visit is focused on provisions—biscuits, rum, bread, rice, three Dutch cheeses, five pieces of dried goat meat, and some corn that had been stored up for the chickens, now also victims. Using the carpenter's chest, Crusoe constructs a raft from planks. This enables him to rescue probably the most important gifts proffered by the wreck—two fowling pieces, two pistols along with much gunpowder and shot. In all these trips he is hampered by the tides, which he has to read carefully, especially as he is unfamiliar with the shore and its sandbars. He climbs to the top of a hill to discover that he is indeed on an island, not the mainland.

Having made a second raft, Crusoe is able to retrieve a great many useful things, which he enumerates in detail:

> I found two or three bags full of nails and spikes, a great screw-jack, a dozen or two of hatchets, and above all, that most useful thing call'd a grind-stone; all of these I secured together, with several things belonging to the gunner, particularly two or three iron crows, and two barrels of musquet-bullets, seven musquets, and another fowling-piece, with Some quantity of powder more; a large bag full of small shot, and a great roll of sheet lead: But this last was so heavy, I could not hoist it up to get it over the ship's side. (44–45)

It is only on his twelfth visit, after thirteen days, that the wind begins to rise. But at low water he is still able to find some razors, scissors, knives, and forks. And in another drawer,

> I found about thirty-six Pounds value in money, some *European* coin, some *Brasil,* some Pieces of Eight, some gold, some silver . . . I smil'd to my self at the sight of this money, O drug! Said I aloud, what art thou good for? Thou art not worth to me, no not the taking off of the ground, one of those knives is worth all this heap . . . However, upon second thoughts I took it away. (47)

With the weather worsening, Crusoe's concerns turn to the construction of a strategically placed shelter and fortification against any wild animals or savages that might inhabit the island. Making a tent from the ship's sails, he labouriously uses its cables and cuts rows of stakes to make a fence over two feet high.

The entrance into this place I made be not by a door, but by a short ladder, to go over the top, which ladder, when I was in, I lifted over after me, and so I was completely fenced in, and fortify'd, as I thought, from all the world, and consequently slept secure in the night, which otherwise I would not have done, tho' as it appear'd afterward, there was no need of all this caution from the enemies I apprehended danger from . . . Into this fence or fortress, with infinite labour, I carri'd all my riches, all my provisions, ammunition and stores, of which you have the account above. (49)

A storm alerts Crusoe to the danger of hoarding all his powder together, so he divides it into a hundred separate packs, which takes him a fortnight to distribute in safe places. In this time he discovers that the island is inhabited by goats, which he learns to track and kill, using a cave he had excavated behind his tent as a fireplace and then kitchen. He now turns to introspection over his condition:

I had great reason to consider it as a determination of Heaven, that in this desolate place, and in this desolate manner I should end my life; the tears would run plentifully down my face when I made these reflections . . . But something always return'd swift upon me to check these thoughts, and to reprove me . . . Well, you are in a desolate condition, 'tis true, but pray remember, Where are the rest of you? Did you not come eleven of you into the boat, where are the ten? Why were they not sav'd and you lost? (51)

Crusoe begins to reconcile himself to a prolonged stay and to making a record of his experience, cutting notches in a tree to mark the passing of days (with a seventh, larger, for the Sabbath), consulting the books, including three English Bibles, he had retrieved from the wreck, and attending to the dog and two female cats that he had rescued. The dog was a 'trusty servant to me for many years; I wanted nothing that he could fetch me, nor any company that he could make up to me, I only wanted to have him talk to me, but that he would not do' (53). The cats, on the other hand, as he later notes in his journal, began to breed with wild felines, producing so many kittens 'that I was forc'd to kill them like vermin, or wild beasts, and to drive them from my house as much as possible' (82).

Crusoe uses the ink and paper that he has rescued to draw up two columns—'evil' and 'good'—assessing his situation materially and morally, and to start a journal, which he reproduces for us in some detail from 30 September 1659 through to 3 January of the following year, when it is interrupted by his work to strengthen his defences, and from that April until the first anniversary of his arrival, at which point his ink starts to run out. From a combination of the journal and his regular narrative we learn that his regular day would comprise a two or three-hour morning walk (if it did not rain) armed with his gun, then work until around 11, some food at noon, a siesta from 12 to 2, and a return to work in the evening. He admits that sometimes he neglected to mark the Sabbath in his calendar but reports success in taming a kid goat that he had wounded, and, extraordinarily, his discovery of shoots of barley of the English variety. This latter eventuality is the source of renewed puzzlement:

> It is impossible to express the astonishment and confusion of my
> thoughts on this occasion: I had hitherto acted upon no religious
> foundation at all, indeed I had very few notions of religion in my
> head . . . But after I saw barley grow there . . . I began to suggest
> that God had miraculously caus'd this grain to grow without any
> help of seed sown . . . [but] it occurr'd to my thoughts, that I had
> shook a bag of chickens meat out in that place, and then the won-
> der began to cease; and I must confess, my religious thankfulness
> to God's Providence began to abate . . . upon the discovering that
> all this was nothing but what was common. (63–64)

And so, when shortly afterwards the island is hit by an earthquake and
hurricane, Crusoe likewise admits that his pleas to the Lord to save him
are prayers of a purely reflexive type, unable to release him from a constant
fear of being swallowed up by the earth or rock falls. In May and June he
returned to the wreck, to strip it of timber before falling ill. Again, Crusoe
prays to God but is in such a fever that he 'scarce knew what I said, or why;
my thoughts being all confused' (70). Five days later, he starts to recover
but is unable to leave his home to get some rainwater. Falling asleep again,
he has a vivid dream, in which he is sitting on the outside of his wall, just
as after the earthquake, and

> I saw a man descend from a great black cloud, in a bright flame
> of fire, and light upon the ground: He was all over as bright as a
> flame, so that I could but just bear to look towards him; his coun-
> tenance was most inexpressibly dreadful, impossible for words to

describe . . . He was no sooner landed upon the earth, but he mov'd forward towards me, with a long spear or weapon in his hand, to kill me; and when he came to a rising ground, at some distance, he spoke to me, or I heard a voice so terrible, that it is impossible to express the terror of it; all that I can say I understood was this, *Seeing all these things have not brought thee to repentance, now thou shalt die* . . . (70–71)

Afflicted in ways he says he cannot express, Crusoe reflects with anguish that over the previous eight years,

I was merely thoughtless of a God, or a Providence, acted like a meer brute from the principles of Nature, and by the dictates of common sense only, and indeed hardly that. (71)

He returns us to his journal to record his embracing of faith in God and his remembrance of all the moments in which he had been mysteriously spared. Dazed by chewing tobacco soaked in rum, he begins to read one of his three Bibles; the first words that come to eye from Psalm 50: '*Call on me in the day of trouble, and I will deliver, and thou shalt glorify me*' (75). There begins a regular regime of Bible-reading until, in July, Crusoe resolves to explore his island further, taking a three-day journey, during which he discovers a 'delicious vale on the other side, replete with fruit and cocoa trees and fresh water'. He admits to 'a secret kind of pleasure . . . that I was king and lord of all this country indefeasibly, and had a right of possession; and if I could convey it, I might have it in inheritance, as completely as any lord of a manor in England'. (80)

But he returns to his 'home' in the stockade tent, and resolves to keep it as his principal abode. There he spends his second year beginning a cycle of sowing, measuring the seasons by the positions of the sun, starting to weave baskets, and domesticating a young parrot that, in time, needed no cage, but took years to 'talk'. In this, his third year, Crusoe's daily round started with a reading of the scriptures, and took in more curing, preserving, and cooking than before. It takes him forty-two days to make a shelf; he has to ward birds off his barley crop with gunshots and scarecrows, but there is compensation in his parrot learning to speak, uttering 'POLL, which was the first word I ever heard spoken in the island by any mouth but my own' (95).

It is at this stage that Crusoe confronts three serious challenges to his ingenuity and untrained manual skills—the making of clay pots for wet and dry storage, the baking of bread from his barley, and the construction of a canoe that might permit him to travel around the island by sea. The first was imperfectly achieved—'I could not make above two large earthen ugly things, I cannot call them jars, in about two months labour' (96). And, by chance, he learns how to fire his 'pipkins'. The bread, of course, had to be made without yeast, but could be baked with the pots, so Crusoe was able to calculate that his yearly subsistence needs were forty bushels of barley and rice, providing a useful horizon for his planting and retention of seeds. The construction of a large canoe proffered the chance for escape, at least to the mainland. But Crusoe miscalculated hugely by designing a boat out of a large tree, so that when he had spent six months hacking it out—which he admits is not the way the Indians constructed their craft—he found it far too heavy to be moved even a hundred yards to the water. At the end of his fourth year on the island,

> I look'd now upon the world as a thing remote, which I had nothing to do with, no expectation from, and indeed no desires about . . . and well might I say, as Father *Abraham* to *Dives, Between thee and me there is a great gulph fixed* . . . In the first place, I was removed from all the wickedness of the world here: I had neither the *lust of the flesh, the lust of the eye, or the pride of life* [1 John 2:16]. (102)

His personal assessment is still measured—he has enough to eat, and 'I had no room for desire, except it was of things which I had not, and . . . I had, as hinted before, a parcel of money, as well gold as silver, about thirty-six pounds sterling: Alas! There the nasty sorry useless stuff lay; I had no manner of business for it' (103).

Truly out of the world of the cash nexus, Crusoe again seeks a state of equanimity by rehearsing not only the constituents of his earlier 'good column' but also their source in God's Providence. His ink, he reports, is now gone, and so are his linen clothes.

> Tho' it is true, that the weather was so violent hot that there was no need for clothes, yet I could not go quite naked; no, tho' I had been inclined to it, which I was not, nor could not abide the thoughts of it, tho' I was all alone. (107)

Accordingly, being a 'worse tayler' than carpenter, he 'botches' a hat, suit of clothes, and umbrella from the skins of goat kids. For the next five years, 'I cannot say . . . any extraordinary thing happen'd to me':

> Thus, I liv'd mighty comfortably, my mind being entirely composed by resigning to the will of God, and throwing myself wholly upon the disposal of his Providence. This made my life better than sociable; for when I began to regret the want of conversation, I would ask myself, whether thus conversing mutually with my own thoughts and, as I hope I may say, with even God himself by ejaculations, was not better than the utmost enjoyment of human society in the world. (108)

Moreover, taught a severe lesson by the failed canoe, he succeeds in constructing a smaller craft that enables him to return to maritime activity, albeit just around the coast of the island, but even there adverse tides, unexpected currents, and bad weather posed a serious threat, which once nearly took Crusoe's life before he could navigate his 'frigate' to safety. On that occasion, returning, exhausted, from his 'country home' to his stockade, he fell into a deep sleep, only to be awakened 'By a voice calling me by my name several times, *Robin, Robin, Robin Crusoe*, poor *Robin Crusoe*, where are you *Robin Crusoe*? Where are you? Where have you been?' (113) It seemed a dream, only for him to awake to the sight of Poll, who had been repeating 'the bemoaning language' that he had been taught.

Such small but telling incidents cropped up over the following years, as Crusoe improves his pottery with a wheel, makes a pipe, and, in the face of reduced stocks of gunpowder, embarks on a major regime of taming a herd of goats rather than relying upon hunting. In two years he has a herd of forty, and a regular supply of milk, butter, and cheese. This prompts him not only to give thanks to the mercies of his Creator but also to reflect on the familiar and temporal condition that he was now enjoying:

> It would have made a Stoick smile to have seen me and my little family sit down to dinner; there was my majesty the prince and lord of the whole island; I had the lives of my subjects at my absolute command. I could hang, draw, give liberty, and take it away, and no rebels among my subjects. (118)

Further sustained by a regular supply of raisins, stored through the winter, 'as the best and most agreeable dainty of my whole diet' (122), Crusoe reckons that he could happily subsist for forty years beyond the fifteen over which he has occupied the island. 'But now I come to a new scene of my life' (122).

*

> It happen'd one day about noon going towards my boat, I was exceedingly supris'd with the print of a man's naked foot on the shore, which was very plain to be seen in the sand: I stood like one thunderstruck, or as if I had seen an apparition; I listen'd, I look'd round me, I could hear nothing, nor see any thing . . . I went to see if there were any more, and to observe if it might not be my fancy; but there was no room for that, for there was exactly the very

print of a foot, toes, heel, and every part of a foot . . . after innumerable fluttering thoughts, like a man perfectly confus'd and out of myself, I came home to my fortification, not feeling, as we say, the ground I went on, but terrify'd to the last degree, looking behind me at every two or three steps, mistaking every bush and tree, and fancying every stump at a distance to be a man. (122)

Clambering back into his 'castle' by the ladder, Crusoe remembers that he entered the cave at the back, and then nothing more although he was incapable of sleep that night. Whether the solitary footprint was that of the Devil or a savage, his fears momentarily banished his religious hope and 'former confidence in God' (123). He stays inside for three days, building up courage to venture out, not least because the goats need milking. During this time it occurs to him that the footprint might be his own, but when he finally goes out to test that idea, he finds that the print is larger than his foot. The simple fact is 'that some man or men had been on shore' (126).

In what appears to approximate to a panic attack, Crusoe resolves to hide by destroying his enclosures, dispersing his animals and removing all trace of his existence in order that the savages might not seek him out. All of this when

my head was full of vapours . . . fear of danger is ten thousand times more terrifying than danger it self, when apparent to the eye; and we find the burthen of anxiety greater by much, than the evil which we are anxious about. (126)

Gradually recovering from his fright, Crusoe reverses course in deciding to construct a second fortification around his home by planting a grove of trees outside his wall. This is his main preoccupation for five or six years, two of which were dominated by fear of the footprint. He confesses that his prayers to God are primarily motivated by fear, but reflects that Providence had protected him by placing him on the other side of the island from that presumably frequented by the savages. And so it proved to be. Crossing to the southwest point and descending to the shore,

> I was perfectly confounded and amaz'd; nor is it possible for me to express the horror of my mind, at seeing the shore spread with skulls, hands, feet and other bones of human bodies . . . my stomach grew sick, and I was at the point of fainting, when Nature discharg'd the disorder from my stomach; and having vomited with an uncommon violence, I was a little relieved, but could not bear to stay in the place a moment . . . (130–131)

Not daring to go beyond his home, his 'country seat', and the enclosure for the goats for a full two years, Crusoe stopped firing his gun during this period, dreaming of ways in which he might blow up the cannibals— perhaps twenty or thirty of them—with his gunpowder. But after such reveries, he enters into a period of reflection over these passionate reactions,

> And I began with cooler and calmer thoughts to consider what it was I was going to engage in. What authority or call I had, to pretend to be judge and executioner upon these men as criminals,

whom Heaven had thought fit for so many ages to suffer unpun-ish'd, to go on, and to be, as it were, the executioners of his judge-ments upon one another. How far these people were offenders against me, and what right I had to engage in the quarrel of that blood, which they shed promiscuously one upon another. (135)

Not only had the savages inflicted no injury upon Crusoe, but they did not even have knowledge of his existence. Moreover, if he were to attack them, it would be effectively to justify the barbarities practised by the Spaniards in the Americas. The only proper grounds for force would be self-defence. Until that was enforced upon him, the cannibals were effectively innocent, their only crimes being 'national' and so subject to the justice of God, the governor of nations. And Crusoe accordingly gives thanks to God, beseeching him for the protection of Providence from the savages as a kind of exchange for his delivery from 'blood-guiltiness' (137).

Over the months that follow, Crusoe exists in a continued state of anx-iety, quietly going about his activities alert to any 'secret dictate' whereby God might be guiding him through natural intuition, which he unerringly obeyed. This does not, however, protect him from fright and delusion when, cutting through some brushwood in front of a cave, 'I saw two broad shin-ing eyes of some creature, whether Devil or man I knew not' (140). But they are those of an old goat, 'just making his will, as we say, and gasping for life, and dying indeed of meer old age'. (141) The next day he buries the goat, and even as he continues to prepare his ordnance for any coming encounter with the savages, he reflects that Poll lived with him for over twenty years, the dog, 'a very pleasant and loving companion' dying at sixteen of 'meer old age' whilst Crusoe continues to cull the population of cats, bar 'two or three favourites' (143). He has been a castaway for twenty-three years.

It is December, and harvesttime, when the savages appear on Crusoe's side of the island. Initially, he flees back to his fortification and prepares his muskets. But after a couple of hours, he realises the shortcomings of this response since he needed to know what was happening outside and 'had no spies to send out' (144). Again, once the cannibals have departed in their canoes on the tide, he finds the ghastly detritus of their feast. And Crusoe again muses that 'the expectation of evil is more bitter than the suffering', and that he would be best off developing a plan to deal with the savages, rather than dwelling on his emotional response to them. They do not reappear for another fifteen months, but he continues to dream of them, and of killing them.

In May of Crusoe's twenty-fourth year his reading of the Bible is interrupted by the sound of a gun firing, apparently at sea, and so likely to be from a ship in distress. The next morning that sorry apprehension is borne out by the sight of a wreck on the rocks, exciting all sorts of scenarios in Crusoe's mind as to how it might have been brought about, and, just as importantly, how close he had come to restoring human companionship. He was not sure if there were any survivors, finding only the corpse of the ship's boy, but even this has less impact than the loss of company:

> *O, that it had been but one!* I believe that I repeated the words, *O that it had been but one!* A thousand times; and the desires were so

mov'd by it, that when I spoke the words, my hands would clinch together, and my fingers press the palms of my hands, that if I had any soft thing in my hand, it would have crush'd it involuntarily; and my teeth in my head would strike together, and set against one another so strong, that for some time I could not part them again. (149)

The state of the sea impedes Crusoe from boarding the wreck for a while, but when he manages this, he finds a dog that is just alive, two men clinging to each other in death, two cases that he can unload, twenty gallons of rum, and some fine clothing. And, as in the case of his own ship a full quarter century earlier,

> I found there three great bags of Pieces of Eight, which held about eleven hundred Pieces in all; and in one of them, wrapt up in a paper, six Doubloons of gold and some small bars or wedges of gold; I suppose they might all weigh near a pound. (152)

This would be in keeping with a ship travelling from Buenos Aires or Brazil to Havana. Crusoe, of course, 'had no manner of occasion' for the money, which he would readily have exchanged for three or four pairs of English shoes—the dead sailors wearing 'what we call pumps, than shoes'—but he still lugged the cash to his cave. Nothing else seemed to have changed; his rhythm of life resumed, and he avoided leaving his side of the island. However, he is troubled by the thought that if he had stayed in Brazil all those years ago, he might by now have made a fortune of 100,000 *Moydors*, and he muses on the relative ease of mind in the early years, before he knew of the existence of cannibals who 'thought it no more a crime to kill and devour me, than I did of a pigeon, or a curlieu' (155). It is with such thoughts in his mind, that the agitated Crusoe falls into a deep sleep and experiences a vivid dream of a prisoner of the cannibals escaping from them on the shore and running into his grove to hide; 'He kneel'd down to me, seeming to pray me to assist him; upon which I shew'd my ladder, made him go up, and carry'd him into my cave; and he became my servant' (157).

The upshot of this dream is that Crusoe decides his only chance of escape from the island is to secure the support of one of the savages, even if this would prove very difficult in practical terms. But it does alter his entire attitude to their visits, which he now anticipates with some keenness. It is a full eighteen months before one does occur, and it involves five canoes, with over twenty men. Crusoe does not go out, but he does ready his defences and observes the developing feast closely, one of two prisoners being killed and prepared for the meal.

The other, sensing the distraction,

> Started away from them, and ran with incredible swiftness along the sands directly towards me . . . I was dreadfully frighted (that I must acknowledge) when I perceived him to run my way . . . However, I kept my station, and my spirits began to recover, when I found that there was not above three men that follow'd him; and

still more was I encourag'd when I found that he outstript them
exceedingly in running . . . (159)

Crusoe collects his guns, runs between the victim and his pursuers, one of
whom he knocks down with the butt of the musket, so as not to alert the
main group. However, the other has a bow and arrow,

so I was then necessitated to shoot him first, which I did, and
kill'd him at the first shoot; the poor savage who fled, but had
stopp'd . . . came nearer and nearer, kneeling down every ten or
twelve steps, in token of acknowledgement for my saving his life:
I smil'd at him, and look'd pleasantly, and beckon'd to him to
come still nearer; at length he came close to me, and then kneel'd
down again, and laid his head upon the ground, and taking me by
the foot, set my foot upon his head; this, it seems, was in token of
swearing to be my slave forever . . . (161)

So it is that Crusoe hears the first human voice other than his own for
twenty-five years, but, of course, the two cannot understand each other
through words. Nevertheless, the new slave is able to indicate that he needs
Crusoe's sword to deal with the wounded savage, and 'he no sooner had it,
but he runs to his enemy, and at one blow cut off his head as cleaverly, no
executioner in *Germany*, could have done it sooner or better' (161). Together
they bury the two corpses, Crusoe provides his slave with bread, raisins,
and fresh water, and then encourages him to go to sleep. This enables the
castaway to take physical stock of his new companion.

He was a comely, handsome fellow, perfectly well made, with straight strong limbs, not too large; tall and well shap'd, and, as I reckon, about twenty-six years of age. He had a very good countenance, not a fierce and surly aspect, but seem'd to have something very manly in his face, and yet he had all the sweetness and softness of an *European* in his countenance too, especially when he smil'd. His hair was long and black, not curl'd like wool; his forehead very high, and large, and a great vivacity and sparkling sharpness in his eyes. The colour of his skin was not quite black, but very tawny; and yet not of an ugly yellow and nauseous tawny, as the *Brasilians*, and *Virginians*, and other natives of *America* are . . . His face was round and plump; his nose small, not flat like the negroes, a very good mouth, thin lips, and his fine teeth well set, and white as ivory. (162)

Crusoe, we know, greatly values time as well as words. So, after the savage had indicated through signs that

he would serve me as long as he liv'd . . . I made him know his name should be *Friday*, which was the day I sav'd his life; I call'd him so for the memory of the time. I likewise taught him to say *Master*, and then let him know that was to be my name; I likewise taught him to say, *Yes*, and *No*, and to know the meaning of them. (163)

The relief of survival must have made this an easy step. But a fuller acculturation plainly posed a challenge when Friday suggested that they disinter the buried cannibals and eat them themselves. Appalled by both this and

39

the remnants of the feast, Crusoe makes Friday clear them up, resolved to kill him should he continue with his own cannibalism, and starts to deck him out with some of the linen recovered from the recent wreck as well as goatskin. Friday is to sleep outside the stockade, with ladders still drawn up. But Crusoe soon recognises that all his precautions are unnecessary,

> For never man had a more faithful, loving, sincere servant than *Friday* was to me; without passions, sullenness, or designs, perfectly oblig'd and engag'd; his very affections were ty'd to me, like those of a child to a father; and dare I say, he would have sacrific'd his life for saving mine. (165)

Alongside the challenge of teaching Friday to speak was that of weaning him off an appetite for human flesh, Crusoe shooting a kid for that purpose, although the act only prompted Friday to rip open his waistcoat to see if he himself was wounded and then imploring Crusoe, by hugging his knees, not to shoot him. Even after Crusoe has shot some birds to reveal the mysteries of a firearm, Friday is only partially instructed:

> As for the gun itself, he would not so much as touch it for several days after; but would speak to it, and talk to it, as if it had answer'd him, when he was by himself; which, as I afterwards learn'd of him, was to desire it not to kill him. (167)

The adjustments are not all on the one side. Crusoe has to reacquaint himself with the use of speech as he teaches, which contributed to 'the pleasantest year of all that life I led in this place' (168). Step by step, combining

"Robinson Crusoe and Man Friday" by Carl Offterdinger, 1880.

words, signs, and symbols Friday explains that at cannibal feasts up to twenty victims might be consumed, and that canoes could reach the island with ease, following familiar currents and tides. Crusoe calculates that they are located close to mouth of the River Orinoco, to the southeast of Trinidad, which chimes with the fact that the only intelligible name of local people he can ascertain from Friday is that of the Caribs.

Friday informs his new master of his people's religion based on the venerable *Benamuckee*, older than the sea, the moon, or the stars. And he, in turn,

> listen'd with great attention, and receiv'd with pleasure the notion of *Jesus Christ* . . . I enter'd into a long discourse with him about the Devil, the original of him, his rebellion against God, his enmity to man, the reason of it, his setting himself up in the dark parts of the world to be worship'd instead of God. (171)

But such a figure posed something of a logical problem for Friday.

> Well, says *Friday*, but you say, God is so strong, so great, is he not much strong, much might as the Devil? . . . *if God much strong, much might as the Devil, why God no kill the Devil, so make him no more do wicked?* (172)

In the face of persistent incredulity at his explanations, Crusoe simply effects a practical diversion to stall the mutually unintelligible exchanges, praying to God to help him in the task of securing Friday's religious instruction and redemption. That process, at first so exigent, has by the end of the three years they lived together yielded a thankful result:

We liv'd there together perfectly and compleatly happy, *if any such thing as compleat happiness can be form'd in a sublunary state.* The savage was now a good Christian . . . much better than I. (174)

As Friday's English improves the exchange of information extends beyond the confines of work and worship, Crusoe learning that there are white men—survivors of a shipwreck—living amongst Friday's Carib people, speaking their language, and not vulnerable to being eaten because they were not seen as enemies. Crusoe is taken aback by Friday's desire to go home, but reassured by his parallel wish to do so together with Crusoe and as a civilised Christian ready to assume the tasks of conversion. However, Crusoe is in no state of mind to adopt Carib boat-building techniques as they set about making a craft to take them off the island. Friday, on the other hand, learns how to sail and manage a rudder, and Crusoe continues to attend his normal agricultural activity.

Two weeks before their planned departure, and with stocks prepared for the voyage, Friday, who was out searching for a turtle to kill, comes running back from the shore in a state of high agitation, shouting that three canoes are approaching the beach.

Says I, *Friday, we must resolve to fight them; Can you fight,* Friday? *Me shoot,* says he, *but there come many great number.* No matter for that, said I again, our guns will frighten them that we do not kill . . . He said, *me die, when you bid die, Master.* (182)

Fortified by a strong dram of rum as well as the many firearms they had prepared, Crusoe and Friday prepare an ambush, although Crusoe rehearses his ethical doubts about such an attack on people 'who, as to me, were innocent and whose barbarous customs were their own disaster, being in them a token indeed of God's having left them.' (183)

But such scruples are completely extinguished, when, observing from the woods close to the beach, they see that the first victim is not another Carib but a bearded European. On Crusoe's order Friday opens the firing, killing two savages and wounding three straightaway. Chaos and consternation ensue as the cannibals have no idea whence their destruction comes. Picking up new guns, the pair now run out of the woods and releases the victim, a Spaniard, who, though weak, now joins the fight. The slaughter continues in remorseless fashion even into the sea against those seeking desperately to escape in their canoe. Crusoe carefully lists twenty-one casualties, who killed them, and where they died.

But the encounter is not fully over. For hidden in one of the canoes is a second victim for the planned feast:

> When . . . *Friday* came to hear him speak, and look in his face, it would have mov'd any one to tears, to have seen how *Friday* kiss'd him, embrac'd him, hugg'd him, cry'd, laugh'd, hollow'd, jump'd about, danc'd, sung, then cry'd again, wrung his hands, beat his own face and head . . . It was a good while before I could make him speak to me, or tell what was the matter; but when he came a little to himself, he told me, that it was his father. (187)

This happy family development is matched by a public transformation, Crusoe reflecting,

> My island was now peopled, and I thought my self very rich in subjects; and it was a merry reflection which I frequently made, how like a king I look'd. First of all, the whole country was my own meer property; so that I had an undoubted right of dominion. Secondly, my people were perfectly subjected: I was absolute lord and law-giver; they all ow'd their lives to me . . . It was remarkable too, we had but three subjects, and they were of three different religions. My man *Friday* was a Protestant, his father was a pagan and a *cannibal*, and the Spaniard was a Papist. However, I allow'd liberty of conscience throughout my dominions. But this is by the way. (190)

The burial of the bodies and recovery of the Spaniard and Friday's father effectively draw a line under previous plans as well as the fears that underpinned them. Crusoe learns from the Spaniard that some sixteen of his countrymen and some Portuguese—all victims of the wreck of a ship sailing from the Rio de la Plata to Havana—lived amongst the Caribs but in very straitened circumstances, not even being able to construct a craft to effect their escape. But what if they were to come to Crusoe's island?

> I told him with freedom, I fear'd mostly their treachery and ill usage of me, if I put my life in their hands . . . that I would rather be deliver'd up to the *savages*, and be devour'd alive, than fall

into the merciless claws of the priests, and be carry'd into the *Inquisition* . . . He answer'd with a great deal of candor and inge-nuity . . . he would make conditions with them upon their solemn oath that they should be absolutely under my leading, as their commander and captain; and that they should swear upon the Holy Sacraments and the Gospel, to be true to me, and to go to such Christian country as that I should agree to. (192–193)

Reassured by the promise of such fealty, Crusoe agrees that the Spaniard and Friday's father should make the voyage to the Carib island in order to bring over the Europeans, for whom they spend a month collecting suffi-cient provisions. Crusoe is unsure when exactly they leave, as he has lost confidence in his notched calendar, but he knows that they have been gone eight days when Friday 'came running in and call'd aloud, Master, master, they are come, they are come' (196).

It is not, however, a canoe that he sees. It is an English sailing ship, and it has lowered a longboat that is rowing toward the shore. Crusoe fears the worst as he observes the craft approach, reaffirming his conviction that

Such hints and notices of danger are . . . discoveries of an invisible world, and a converse of spirits . . . and if the tendency of them seems to be to warn us danger, why should we not suppose they are from some friendly agent, whether supreme, or inferior and subordinate . . . ? (197)

Whatever its origin, his intuition proved well founded. Of the eleven men who land, three were plainly prisoners. For Friday this showed that the English ate their captives just like the cannibals, but Crusoe knew about mutinies and now resolved to embark not on a slaughter but a campaign of subterfuge although he and Friday went hidden and as heavily armed as before. At the height of the day, with the sailors sleeping in the woods, the three captives huddled anxiously under a tree are frightened by the sound and even more by the sight of Crusoe as he approaches them through the undergrowth. He explains that he cannot be an angel, still less God, because he is so poorly clothed: 'I am a man, an *English man,* and dispos'd to assist you, you see: I have one servant only; we have arms and ammunition; tell us freely. Can we serve you?—What is your case?' (200)

The captain of the ship explains that he, the ship's mate and a passenger had indeed been made prisoners by the mutineers and that they expected to perish on the island which they imagined to be uninhabited. Crusoe offers his help, but again upon conditions—that they accept his complete authority, that they will return any arms he gives them, that they will do him no prejudice, and that if the ship is recovered, they will give him and Friday free passage to England.

Such terms readily agreed, the subsequent encounter with the rebel group predictably proves to involve violent action, with two being shot dead, another wounded, and one group now lost in the woods. From his captives, Crusoe learns that there are twenty-six men still on the ship, and it is evident that they will come to seek out their co-conspirators who have not returned in the longboat. Over the following hours, Crusoe and his new subjects, including the captured mutineers who now resubmitted themselves to the authority of the captain, play cat-and-mouse with the confused mutineers through verbal and gunshot night-time ambushes in the woodland.

This time both sides are armed and speak the same language; there is disorientation in the dark but also a distinct testing of nerve through deception:

> *For God's sake*, Tom Smith, *throw down your arms, and yield*, or, *you are all dead men this moment . . . Who must we yield to? Where are they? . . . here they are* . . . here's our Captain, and fifty men with him, have been hunting you these two hours; the Boat-swain is kill'd, *Will Frye* is wounded . . . you are all lost . . . Upon this *Will. Atkins* cry'd out, *For God's sake, Captain, give me quarter, what have I done? They have all been as bad as I* . . . In a word, they all laid down their arms, and begg'd their lives . . . I kept my self and one more out of sight, for reasons of state. (210–211)

This charade of an invisible 'Governour' continues for quite a while until the ship is eventually attacked and captured by the captain's force, the adventure being closed with he and Crusoe rejoicing over their deliverance at the hands of each other. The captain orders that the governor be sent gifts from the ship of a type that Crusoe has not savoured for decades and which he now enumerates with precise delight:

First he had brought me a case of bottles full of excellent cordial waters, six large bottles of *Madera* wine; the bottles held two-quarts a-piece; two pound of excellent good tobacco, twelve good pieces of the ship's beef, and six pieces of pork, with a bag of pease, and about a hundred weight of bisket . . . He brought me also a box of sugar, a box of flower, a bag full of lemons, and two bottles of lime-juice, and abundance of other things: But besides these, and what was a thousand times more useful to me, he brought me six clean new shirts, six very good neckclothes, two pairs of gloves, one pair of shoes, a hat, and one pair of stockings, and a very good suit of clothes of his own, which he had worn but very little . . . (215–216)

Crusoe's old world is returning, but for the mutineers that means being hanged at the yard-arm, either in England, to which the captain is pledged to carry Crusoe, or in one of her colonies, through which he is likely to pass. There is a momentary clash of authority between the captain, who commands the vessel and wishes to have the prisoners sent to the gallows, and Crusoe, who stays ashore and says the prisoners are his. He then informs the prisoners that, as governor, he possesses the authority to have them hanged but would extend mercy if they agreed to stay on the island.

Accordingly I gave them the whole history of the place, and of my coming to it; shew'd them my fortifications, the way I made my bread, planted my corn, cured my grapes; and in a word all that was necessary to make them easy: I told them the story also of the sixteen *Spaniards* that were to be expected; for whom I left a letter, and made them promise to treat them in common with themselves. (218)

For mementos of his life as a castaway, Crusoe took with him

> The great goat's-skin-cap I had made, my umbrella, and my parrot; also I forgot not to take the money I formerly mention'd, which had lain by me so long useless, that it was grown rusty, or tarnish'd, and could hardly pass for silver, till it had been a little rubb'd, and handled; as also the money I had found on the wreck of the *Spanish* ship . . . And thus I left the island, the nineteenth of *December*, as I found by the ship's account, in the year 1686, after I had been upon it eight and twenty years, two months, and 19 days; being deliver'd from this second captivity, the same day of the month that I first made my escape in the *barco-longo* from the *Moors* of *Sallee*. (218–219)

*

The story is not yet over. But it is drawing to a close. And it does so at some pace. When Crusoe lands in England on 11 June 1687, he has been away for thirty-five years. So it is no surprise that when he goes to Yorkshire he finds that all his family have died except two sisters and two children of one of his brothers. Since he had long since been given up for dead, he had no family inheritance. But this absence is more than adequately compensated for when he returns to Lisbon, where his partner in Brazil and all who had been his benefactors up to his shipwreck had diligently kept his property in trust, developed his plantation, preserved interest, and notarised his property, notwithstanding his longstanding absence and the reasonable assumption—as made by his family—of his death.

> I was now master, all on a sudden, of above 5000 *l. Sterling* in money, and had an estate, as I might well call it, in the *Brasils*, of above a thousand pounds a year, as sure as an estate of lands in *England*. And in a word, I was in a condition which I scarce knew how to understand, or how to compose myself, for the enjoyment of it. (224)

Crusoe sets about making philanthropic gifts, to his benefactors, business partners, and religious foundations, but amidst this profusion of revenue, he had to admit that

> I had more care upon my head now, than I had in my silent state of life in the island, where I wanted nothing but what I had, and had nothing but what I wanted . . . I had ne'er a cave now to hide my money in, or a place where it might lye without lock or key . . . On the contrary, I knew not where to put it, or who to trust with it. (225)

After a flurry of correspondence in an effort to resolve this challenge, Crusoe sets out from Lisbon with Friday, to return to England. But he is determined to avoid any further prolonged voyage at sea, and so they set out for Calais on horseback in a group including further servants. It is on this final voyage that they encounter an unforgiving natural coda to their life on the island. As they seek to cross the snowbound Pyrenees with the help of a guide, they are attacked three times by ravenous packs of wolves, scores of which are killed as, between gunshots and lighting fires, the embattled group defend their lives until they reach a village on the French side. It is in Europe, not the tropics, where Crusoe comes closest to being devoured by wild animals; and it was in the tropics that he tamed animals such that he lost the intuition—whatever its course—that the wolves were much less interested in eating the humans than the horses they rode.

Crusoe decides that he cannot return to Brazil 'unless I resolv'd to embrace the *Roman* Catholick religion, without any reserve' (238), which he cannot. He sells the plantation for 32,800 pieces of eight, makes more gifts of money and pensions for his benefactors and stays in England.

> In the mean time, I in part settled myself here; for first of all I marry'd and that not either to my disadvantage or dissatisfaction, and had three children, two sons and one daughter. But my wife dying, and my nephew coming home from good success from a voyage to *Spain*, my inclination to go abroad, and his importunity prevailed and engag'd me to go to his ship, as a private trader to the *East Indies*: This was in the year 1694. (240)

Crusoe is some sixty-two years of age. He is now submitting to family encouragement, not rebelling against it. Yet the ending of this tale is not exactly happy, for when he visits the island once more, he finds those who had settled it in a desperate state after Carib invasions and the virtual collapse of their planation.

> All these things, with some very surprising incidents in some new adventures of my own, for ten years more, I may perhaps give a farther account of hereafter. (241)

*

On 20 August 1719, less than three weeks after the issue of the fourth edition of the first volume of *Robinson Crusoe*, Defoe, true to his words in the final paragraph of that volume, published a follow-up: *The Farther Adventures of Robinson Crusoe; Being the Second and Last Part of his Life, and of the Strange Surprizing Accounts of his Travels Round three parts of the Globe*. Although often published together with the original—in the 1888 edition without any break, and in that of 1953 with one simply resembling a new chapter—this book is far less well known than the first.

John Richetti suggests a very good reason why—it lacks 'the clear focus and depth of character development produced by Crusoe's long isolation on the island', because Defoe had opted to pursue the adventure story and travel account of the first book, rather than resume its study in inner development.[1] In pretty much the same vein, Melissa Free notes that the 'Crusoe' that we know only from volume one

> does not fail as a colonial administrator, lose his man Friday, travel to Madagascar, or witness his shipmates (fellow Europeans) 'violate the terms of [a] trade agreement,' then brutally massacre

53

a village there. Nor does he visit the Bay of Bengal, the Malay Archipelago, China, Pekin, Tartary, and Russia; get kicked off his nephew's ship; get mistaken for a pirate; trade with savvy Far Easteners; spew invectives against the Chinese; destroy an idol; decimate a village; run out of unexplored territory; or pale in spiritual comparison to a Russian nobleman, only to return home rich but without family or subject. And finally, he does not declare that 'heaven can gorge us with our own desires'.

Free notes that Dickens found Friday's death—shot by a Carib arrow at sea off the original island, halfway through the text—to be 'one of the least tender and (in the true sense) least sentimental things ever written'.[2] Of course, such a reaction depends upon a close familiarity with the first book, and although the sequel is entirely unworthy of comparison with it in terms of originality, it does in a few respects help our understanding of Defoe's reaction to his recently completed masterpiece.

In the first place, he scrupulously maintained the format of an edited memoir, the preface pungently noting that,

All the endeavours of envious people to reproach it [*Crusoe I*] with being a romance, to search it for errors in geography, inconsistency in the relation, and contradictions in the fact, have proved abortive, and as impotent as malicious.[3]

At almost the same length, the sequel must have been under Defoe's pen from the very moment that *Crusoe I* was published, its author recognising a rich and immediate commercial opportunity even as he sought to settle accounts with his critics. And one senses a certain need to rectify deficiencies in the predecessor. Perhaps one of the most notable of these is in the depiction of matrimonial affairs, so fleetingly dispatched at the start and end of *Crusoe I*. Perhaps a fifth of *Crusoe II* touches directly or indirectly on this theme, as when Crusoe returns to the island, finding its population of both sexes cohabiting without the institution of marriage, which is tolerantly instituted by a French Catholic priest.

Compositionally and ethically more telling is Defoe's return to Crusoe's own wife, whose life and death occupied only two sentences at the end of *Crusoe I*. As we will see, there is a case for thinking that Defoe had his wife, Mary, in mind when he fleshed out the reasons why the death of Crusoe's spouse caused him, aged over sixty, to set out on his travels again:

> When she was gone, the World look'd aukwardly round me; I was as much a stranger in it as I was in Brasils, when I went first on Shore; and as much alone, except as to the Assistance of Servants, as I was on my Island. I knew neither what to do, or what not to do. I saw the World busy around me, one part labouring for Bread, and the other Part squandering in vile Excesses or empty Pleasures, equally miserable, because the End they propos'd still fled from them; for the Man of Pleasure every Day surfeited his Vice, and heaped up Work for Sorrow and Repentance; and the Men of labour spent their Strength in daily strugglings for Bread to maintain the vital Strength they labour'd with, so living in a daily Circulation of Sorrow, living but to work, and working but

to live, as if daily Bread were the only End of wearisome Life, and a wearisome Life the only Occasion of daily Bread. (255)

Rarely has personal grief morphed so fluently into social critique. Although Karl Marx would focus his usage of Crusoe on the first volume and against the classical economists' insistence on ignoring society and history or, like Ricardo, applying them anachronistically, here Defoe's supra-Puritanism anticipates nineteenth-century radicalism in a way that Marx allowed, as in the case of *Don Quixote*.[4]

Defoe goes a bit further still, setting the loss of his wife against the backdrop of a settled and comfortable existence depicted by Crusoe's father as the epitome of the 'middle station' and from which the younger man had run away to sea:

I farm'd upon my own land, I had no rent to pay, was limited by no articles; I could pull up or cut down as I pleased: what I planted was for my self, and what I improved was for my family; and having thus left off the thoughts of wandring, I had not the least discomfort in any part of life, as to this world. Now I thought indeed that I enjoyed the middle state of life that my father so earnestly recommended to me, and liv'd a kind of heavenly life ... (254)

As Richetti has noted, in his second volume Defoe also appears to be honing both his observational technique and ambivalence about violence visited upon foreign people. When his partner's ship is being caulked in

Indo China it is attacked by local people who are repelled by the carpenter drenching them in boiling pitch. The natives

> made such a howling and crying, that I never heard a worse noise, and, indeed, nothing like it; for it is worth observing, that though pain naturally makes all people cry out, yet every nation has a particular way of exclamation, and making noises as different as one another as their speech . . . I never heard any Thing more like the noise of the wolves, which, as I have said, I heard how in the forest on the frontiers of Languedoc . . . I was sick of killing such poor savage wretches, even though it was in my own defence, knowing they came on errands which they thought just, and knew no better; and that though it may be a just thing, because necessary, for there is no necessary wickedness in nature; yet I thought it was a sad life in which we must be always obliged to be killing our fellow-creatures to preserve our own . . . (406)

One can here see prefigured Martin Green's thesis that the passage of the early English novel would over subsequent decades be away from foreign adventure towards personal affairs at home because such imperial violence was simply too raw for a reading public of 'the middle state'.[5]

One of the central metaphors of *Crusoe I* was that of kingship, returned to some seven times—occasionally with irony as when the subjects are animals or there is no rival or even no subject at all—and often taken as one of the book's core political allegories. In the sequel this figure is effectively effaced. The colonial order on the island in the final passages of the first text has not just fallen prey to invasion and internal dissension; Crusoe admits that he messed up in the way he left it and treated it from afar. At the end of *Crusoe II* we have been transported to Siberia, where Crusoe encounters a prince who has been banished into exile. The traveller offers to smuggle him back to freedom in his caravan, but the nobleman rejects the offer with a wilful repudiation of worldly greatness that echoes Crusoe's own reflections on the qualities of freedom:

> Here I am, free from the temptation of returning to my former miserable greatness; there I am not sure but that all the seeds of pride, ambition, avarice and luxury, which I know remain in nature, may revive and take root, and in a word, again overwhelm me; and then the happy prisoner, whom you see now master of his soul's liberty, shall be the slave of his own senses, in the full of all personal liberty. (458)

And so it is that Crusoe, having tarried on his way back in Hamburg and The Hague, prepares his reader for closure around the unfamiliar—and un-Puritan—theme of retirement at home:

> And here, resolving to harass my self no more, I am preparing for a longer journey than all these, having liv'd 72 years, a life of infinite variety, and learn'd sufficiently to know the value of retirement, and the blessing of ending our days in peace. (468)

*

And there, one feels, Crusoe's story should finally end. And in a sense it does because there is no substantive narrative development in the third volume, *Serious Reflections during the Life and Surprising Adventures of Robinson Crusoe: with his Vision of the Angelick World*, published on 6 August 1720. What we will call *Crusoe III* is hardly ever read today, and it shows every sign of being written largely to cash in on the popularity of the original, which would go into its fifth edition the following November. At some 350 pages, *Crusoe III* is a very serious ramble across a series of themes, the first of which, solitude, is plausibly linked to the initial script. Thereafter, however, 'Crusoe' discourses liberally about honesty, 'the *Immorality of* Conversation, and *The Vulgar* Errors of *Behaviour*', adding an essay on the present state of religion in the world, and others on listening to the voice of Providence, and the proportion between the Christian and the Pagan world. Finally, over the course of more than 80 (separately numbered) pages, *Vision of the Angelick World* takes readers not just inside Crusoe's mind but far into outer space, with the injunction not to flatter themselves that

> those regions are uninhabited, because the planets appear to be so. No, no, I assure you this is that World of Spirits, or at least is a World of Spirits . . . Here I saw a clear Demonstration of Satan being *the Prince of the Power of the Air*; 'tis in this boundless waste he is confined, whether it be his busie restless Inclination has posted him here, that he may affront God in his Government of the World, and do Injury to Mankind in meer Envy to his Happiness, as the fam'd Mr *Milton* says it, or whether it is that by the eternal Decree

of Providence he is appointed to be Man's continual Disturber for Divine Ends, to us unknown; this I had not wandered far enough to be informed of; those Secrets being lodged much higher, than imagination itself ever travelled. (32)

Perhaps, indeed, it is the reach as much as the limit of imagination that is in play here since a few pages earlier Crusoe proffers a caution to

all vapourish melancholy People, whose Imaginations run this Way; I mean about seeing the Devil, Apparitions and the like; namely, that they should never look behind them, and over their Shoulders as they go up Stairs, or look into the Corners and Holes of Rooms with a Candle in their hands, or turn about to see who might be behind them in any Walks or dark Fields, Lanes, or the like; for let such know, they will see the Devil whether he be there or no; they will be so perswaded that they do see him, that their very Imagination will be a Devil to them where-ever they go. (12)

By this stage the solving and re-setting of riddles has become tiresome, even boorish. Yet at the start of the volume we encounter a new permutation of the now familiar protestations of authenticity. Asserting that 'the Fable is always made for the Moral, not the Moral for the Fable', Crusoe asserts that the story

though Allegorical, is also Historical . . . Farther, that there is a Man alive, and well known too, the Actions of whose life are the just Subject of these Volumes, and to whom, all or most Part of

the Story most directly alludes, this may be depended upon for
Truth and to this I set my name. (2–3)

Since, as we shall see, Defoe had been 'outed' as its author within days of
publication of the first volume, this third denial constitutes something of a
taunt, and one that was surely sharpened by the comparison he then made
between *Crusoe* and *Don Quixote*. Alerted to the sense that this volume will
be more an explication than an evolution of the previous two, we are told a
couple pages further on ''tis as reasonable to represent one kind of imprisonment by another, as it is to represent anything that really exists by that
which exists not'—words quoted by Albert Camus as the epigraph to his
novel *The Plague*. We are, then, confronted with rather more than an authorial vanity—anonymity was a justified and enduring feature of Defoe's literary and other lives—and will need to return to his theory as well as use of
words. First, though, there are the important matters of where the Crusoe
story might have originated and how it was received.

The Story—Sources and Reception

In November 1731, some six months after the death of Daniel Defoe, the
bookseller Olive Payne issued a catalogue of books from his library to be
sold at Round Court, off the Strand. We have very few sources on Defoe's
personal life after *The Appeal to Honour* of 1715 beyond the habitual court
cases for debt and a dozen letters written over the years following the publication of *Crusoe*. So, the Olive Payne catalogue of 1,754 titles should provide
some key information as to our author's tastes and influences. However,

there are a number of problems. First, the seller combined Defoe's library with that of the late Reverend Philips Farewell, Fellow of Trinity College, Cambridge, without indicating what books came from which collection. Secondly, it was the custom of the day to 'salt' collections for sale with other titles that the bookseller wanted to shift, whether or not they belonged to the library advertised. And thirdly, even allowing for the fact that Defoe was as likely as the late divine to have owned some devotional and theological tomes, the catalogue contained at most twenty-five and more probably only a dozen works attributed to Daniel Defoe. Certainly, there was no copy of *Crusoe*. It seems likely that prior to his death Defoe had passed on to Henry Baker, the husband of his favourite daughter Sophia and a keen bibliophile, some part of his library, although when Baker's books were in turn auctioned in 1772, no indication was given of which might have been inherited from his father-in-law. Since the 1731 catalogue was discovered in 1895 by George Aitken—a surname that threads through our story—scholars have been flexing their powers of detection and disputation. Luckily, others, like Diana Souhami and Tim Severin, have done vital island-hopping as well as text truffling so that we now have a plausible picture of the various influences on the composition of *Robinson Crusoe*.[6]

First and most simply, the Olive Payne catalogue lists the 1699 edition of *The Buccaneers of America* by A.O. Exquemelin, who mentions the stranding of 'Will', a Miskito Indian from Nicaragua, on the Pacific island of Juan Fernández, off the coast of Chile. Will, who Severin suggests provides something of a model for Friday, had been marooned when the buccaneer squadron he was accompanying as a fisherman fled the island at the sight of Spanish ships whilst he was hunting goats inland. It was not for a full three years that another English ship, the *Batchelor's Delight*, also a privateer raiding the coasts of Spain's American empire, found and rescued him in 1684. We have an account of Will by the famed mariner William Dampier, who was part of the same squadron and whose *A New Voyage Round the World* was published in 1697 to popular acclaim and which, although not in the 1731 catalogue, would surely have been known to Defoe.

Dampier does not describe Will personally but characterises all Moskito men as 'tall, well made, raw-bon'd, lusty, strong, and nimble of Foot, long-visaged, lank black Hair, took stern, hard favour'd, and of a dark Copper-colour Complexion'.[7] Not only does this seem close to Defoe's description of Friday, but that in turn bore some resemblance to the depiction of Oroonoko, the African prince enslaved in Surinam in Aphra Behn's 1688 novel of the same name: 'His eyes were the most awful that could be seen, and very piercing . . . the white of them being like snow, as were his teeth . . . His nose was rising and Roman, instead of African and flat . . . His hair came down to his shoulders . . . by keeping it combed.' [8]

Perhaps the clinching element in this connection, however, is the fact that in 1684 the *Batchelor's Delight* had amongst its own crew another Miskito, by the name of Robin. This Robin was on the ship's boat when it reached Will on the beach, running towards his fellow native American and throwing himself on the ground in front of him. After Will picked him up and embraced him, he himself fell to the ground in grateful salutation. Dampier notes, 'We stood with pleasure to behold the surprize, and tenderness, and solemnity of this interview which was exceedingly affectionate on both sides. And when their Ceremonies of Civility were over, drew near.'[9] It is not so hard to see in this scene some model for the meeting between Friday and his father described by Defoe over twenty years later.

If Will works well enough for Friday, there is much wider identification of the person of Alexander Selkirk with Robinson Crusoe himself. Again, the castaway is on the Pacific island of Juan Fernández, and once again there is a connection. William Dampier was a commander in squadrons involved both with Selkirk's original landing, at his own request, from the *Cinque Ports* in September 1704, and with his rescue by the *Duke*, under the command of Woodes Rogers in February 1709. Rogers gives a brief but vivid account of Selkirk's experience in his *A Cruising Voyage Round the World*, published in 1712 and not in the Olive Payne catalogue, which does however include the political writings of Richard Steele, who printed an interview with Selkirk in his magazine *The Englishman* in December 1713. Severin is not sure if this is authentic, and it does quite closely resemble Rogers's account, but in any event, Defoe, who had just completed nine years as a journalist specialising in political and international affairs may be expected to be familiar with both accounts.

Rogers and Steele alike indicate at the outset that Selkirk, evidently a strong-willed man as well as an accomplished navigator, had fallen out with the commander of the *Cinque Ports*, Thomas Stradling, over his refusal to dock the ship for repairs. Born in Nether Largo, Fife, in 1680 of Presbyterian stock, Selkirk was in trouble with his church for 'indecent beaiviar' by 1695, but he could not be brought before the Parish since he had run away to sea.[10] As sailing master of the *Cinque Ports*, which carried British letters of marque authorising its raids on Spanish settlements, Selkirk was at some risk of being accused of mutiny, and once landed, of course, he was prey to capture by Spanish forces, only three hundred miles away on the South American mainland. But Stradling was unpopular with his entire crew, and Selkirk was put ashore with supplies sufficient to tide him over at least for a few weeks. Later, spotted by Spanish sailors, who also used Juan Fernández as a source of fresh water, goat-meat, and citrus fruit, he was able to escape by hiding up a tree.

If Defoe was indeed familiar with the accounts of both the mariner Rogers and the journalist Steele, he seems to have followed the latter in his inventory precision:

> He was put ashore from a leaky Vessel, with the Captain of which he had an irreconcileable difference; and he chose rather to take his Fate in this place, than in a crazy Vessel, under a disagreeable Commander. His portion were a Sea Chest, his wearing Cloaths and Bedding, a Fire-lock, a Pound of Gun-powder, a large quantity of Bullets, Flint and Steel, a few pounds of Tobacco, an Hatchet, a Knife, a Kettle, a Bible, and other Books of Devotion, together with Pieces that concerned Navigation and his Mathematical Instruments.[11]

Maybe Steele borrowed this list from Rogers, but if so he added a few items for effect. Both sources, moreover, concur over the fact that Selkirk lived off goats, killing upwards of five hundred, first with his musket, then by hunting them down by foot, then by wounding kids so that they grew up lame and tame. As his linen clothes wore out, he stitched himself a suit of goatskins with a nail. Equally, Selkirk tamed cats to rid himself of a plague of rats, dancing and singing with these cats and the tame goats, in Rogers's words, 'to divert himself . . . So that by the Care of Providence and Vigour of his Youth, being now but about 30 years, he came at last to conquer all the Inconveniences of his Solitude, and to be very easy'. Souhami, who visited the island and talked to its inhabitants in the 1990s, interprets this, not implausibly but with a certain authorial appetite, as masturbating

> against palm trees . . . [and] fucking goats . . . Fucking goats was perhaps less satisfying than the buggery and prostitution of shipboard life, the black misses of heathen ports. It lacked fraternal exchange. But Selkirk was an abandoned man.[12]

Defoe, unsurprisingly, was on public record for his disapproval of masturbation, and even in *Roxana*, which involves some pretty choice voyeurism, sexual matters are only alluded to at second, delicate remove.[13] Still, myth or not, *Crusoe* is nowadays so widely taught in the well-mown campuses of the North that it would be something of a travesty if sexuality were not fully addressed, albeit sometimes with the inventiveness of a faculty more entranced with its own imagination than experienced in the basic mechanics of zoophilia.

But before we return to this salient issue, we should at least complete the sad story of Alexander Selkirk, who returned to Largo a rich man as a result of the privateering success of Rogers's squadron, which succeeded in capturing the galleon *Nuestra Señora de Encarnación y Desengaño* off the

Mexican coast and netted plunder to the tune of almost £150,000, worth well over £20 million in the prices of 2018. As ever in such cases, there were protracted law cases between the crews and sponsors of these privateering enterprises, and Selkirk, never an emollient character, got into trouble soon after he returned to Britain after over eight years abroad. Suspected locally of bigamy and charged with violent behaviour once more, this heavy drinker eventually expired off the coast of West Africa at the age of forty-one still owed bounty of £35.15.9 (35 pounds, 15 shillings, and 9 pence) as, in something of a paradox, he now served in the Royal Navy on anti-pirate duty.

Of course, *Crusoe* was then available in all three volumes, and if Selkirk had the opportunity to read the first, he would have found similarities with his own experience in more than the animal company, clothing, and fear of wild animals. Crusoe, like him, climbed hills, lit beacons, kept two huts with one as a kitchen, suffered from melancholy and sought to escape it in reading the Bible and communing with God. Tim Severin, who, like Souhami, visited Juan Fernández, accepts that Selkirk forms a key element in a composite Crusoe. But he also notes that the island has no turtles—it no longer has any goats after the Chilean ranger service culled them all in 1977—and that Selkirk never inhabited a cave, which is the centrepiece of Crusoe's world. Moreover, Selkirk was effectively a dissident pirate, not a castaway threatened by both pirates and Carib-cannibals. For that element of Defoe's story Severin has found a rich source in the 36-page booklet *Relation of the great suffering and strange adventures of Henry Pitman, Chirurgeon*, published in June 1689 by John Taylor at the 'Sign of the Ship in St Pauls

The statue of Alexander Selkirk at the site of his house on Main Street, Lower Largo, Fife, Scotland.

Churchyard'. There has to be a spoiler alert here . . . for Severin's keen eying over of the original text revealed that this was the same address of Defoe's publisher, Taylor's son William, some twenty years later. The circle seems to have been closer than one might expect, especially since Pitman, like Defoe, fought for the Duke of Monmouth at Sedgemoor in 1685, but unlike Defoe, he did not escape capture and punishment although he was very lucky not to be accounted amongst the two hundred thirty hanged during Judge George Jeffreys's Bloody Assizes.

Pitman was transported to Barbados for ten years as a rebel, and he appears to have received no special treatment for being a surgeon. Like Crusoe's escape from Sallee with Xury, Pitman eventually gets away in a small boat, albeit under cover of night and with a clutch of fellow rebel transportees. The supplies they amass are quite similar, although Crusoe loads beeswax whereas Pitman stocks up on finished candles. Pitman's clandestine journey from Barbados to Salt Tortuga involves storm damage, leakage, and a near-drowning on the coast after a week's voyage. Like Crusoe, the band tires of roast turtle and contrives to fire pots so that they can cook stews and soups. And, of course, they are stranded on an island that is in the Caribbean and not far from the mouth of the River Orinoco. Perhaps, however, the key feature is that he and his companions are detained by a group of pirates, who, keenly conscious that their trade is based on the democracy of spoils as well as voice, refuse to take any of the castaways bar Pitman, valued for his medical skills, aboard their ship.

The final part of the story is recounted months later in a letter to Pitman from fellow maroon John Whicker, who tells of a further pirate visit, a mutiny involving the taking of prisoners, one of whom runs away along the shore not unlike Friday. The maroons ambush the pirates, less violently than do Crusoe and Friday for they lack gunpowder for their muskets, but they are able to take a number of prisoners, seize their vessel, and put them ashore, 'leaving them some of our provisions'. The rebel maroons, who include one Jeremiah Atkins—Defoe's Will Atkins, of course, is left on the island—are able to leave on 24 August 1687, enabling Pitman to include their escape in his *Relation* two years later, and arguably providing Defoe with a plotline for the 'tacked-on' finale for *Crusoe* I. [14]

It is the case that all of these 'inputs' required Defoe's fine-tuned fashioning in order to work as much more than discrete adventure stories. Moreover, they do not provide primary material for central episodes in *Crusoe*—the shipwrecks and the footprint. It is not difficult to find the first of these in Defoe's own experience, when, just released from six months in Newgate Prison for the 'sedition' of his satirical pamphlet *The Shortest-Way with the Dissenters*, he experienced the Great Storm of 26 November 1703. Of the more than eight thousand people who lost their lives in that hurricane, the great majority were seafarers whose vessels were sunk or wrecked on the coast. The following year, Defoe published his first full-length work, *The Storm*, the reportage of which was substantially composed of descriptive letters that he had requested in the press. The book ends with a Lay-Man's Sermon of 20 pages based on the saying in the Old Testament Book of Nahum 'The Lord has his way in the Whirle-Wind and in the Storm, and the Clouds are the Dust of his Feet'.[15]

Three years later one of Defoe's military and political heroes, Sir Cloudesley Shovell, Whig MP for Rochester and Admiral of the Fleet, died with eight hundred men when HMS *Association* was shipwrecked on the rocks off the Isles of Scilly, returning from the campaign off Toulon at a time when there was still no secure means of measuring longitude. Shovell's loss was keenly felt, not only because he was, like Defoe, of modest social background, but also because news of the disaster was accompanied by stories that his body had been swept up on the sands and rifled for valuables by local people. Not quite eaten by cannibals but certainly a violation associated with the savagery of war.[16]

Finally, although Defoe was quite sparing in his quotation of and references to Shakespeare, who did not then enjoy the renown of later epochs, he certainly was familiar with *The Tempest,* which incorporated eyewitness reports of the shipwreck of the *Sea Venture* off Bermuda on its maiden voyage in 1609. A dozen years before he sought a compositional means of getting Crusoe on and off the island, Defoe had discussed the elaborate stage directions of Dryden and Davenant's popular 1675 production of the Shakespeare drama.[17] Of course, Crusoe does not possess Prospero's magical powers, but he does have a very potent book in the Bible, and scores of appearances by 'Providence' definitely play their part.

The footprint episode almost certainly has a deeper, classical origin. In a marginal note to the *Historical Collections* of 1682 that Defoe collated and then presented to Mary Tuffley, whom he would marry two years later, he makes reference to Nicholas Udall's English translation of the *Apophthegmes of Erasmus*. There Erasmus borrows from the Roman historian Vitruvius the story of the shipwrecked Socratic philosopher Aristippus, who, cast ashore on Rhodes, comes across some geometric diagrams drawn in the sand. In Vitruvius's telling, Aristippus sees these as a comforting sign of civilisation—'*hominum enim vestigia video*' (I see the footprints of man). For Stephen Bertman it is not such a leap of imagination for a writer like Defoe to convert such joy into fear and a mark of civilisation into one of savagery, even at the distance of thirty-five years from such a powerful—positively vestigial—image.[18]

Needless to say, there are many further direct and indirect influences suggested, from Homer to Abu Bakr Ibn Tufail's *The History of Hayy Ibn Yaqzan*, wherein a feral child acquires enlightenment alone on a desert island, translated into Latin by Locke's tutor Edward Pococke in 1671, with the English translation of 1711 appearing in the sale of Henry Baker's library. There are stories of castaways in Ceylon (Robert Knox, 1681) and Madagascar (Defoe's Stoke Newington neighbour Robert Drury, who returned in 1717 and whose 1729 *Journal* may have benefited from some local ghost-writing), which have been proposed. Perhaps the most controversial case is that Defoe borrowed liberally from Hendrick Smeek's *The Mighty Kingdom of Krinke Kesmes*, published in the Netherlands in 1708. The Dutch volume comes, though, with edible birds, a footprint (albeit a hopeful one), an intact sea chest, and eventual marriage to a local woman, rather in the style of Will Atkins. The case for plagiarism has been made rather adventurously by the New Zealand scholar David Fausett as a kind of contrarian Southern Seas critique of the mainstream *Crusoe* canon. However, the Fausett thesis does rely on a lot of wishful thinking, not least that Defoe could read Dutch, which is seriously disputed, or that *The Mighty Kingdom* was translated by Robert Harley, the Earl of Oxford, when imprisoned in the Tower, and then smuggled out to Defoe.[19] Suffice it to say, a lot went into *Robinson Crusoe* but a great deal—real and imagined—did not, as well.

*

Defoe had barely started to denounce the piratical version of *Crusoe* when the first substantial critique appeared—*The Life and Strange Surprizing Adventures of Mr D..... De F..., of London, Hosier*—on 28 September 1719. Printed by James Roberts, who had previously worked for Defoe, and priced at one shilling, this 70-page part parody and part critique imitated *Crusoe* from the elaborate title page onwards.[20] Although anonymous, it was widely recognised to be the work of Charles Gildon (1665–1724), who was more of a grub-street hack than Defoe himself and correspondingly less favoured by government largesse, although he had sought that with equal alacrity. Raised a Roman Catholic and educated in Douai, Gildon promoted the Deist cause in the 1690s, and was by 1719 comfortable in dissecting almost any doctrinal deficiency. However, he was most accomplished at direct, personal invective, as in his 1721 description of Alexander Pope (deformed by a childhood illness) as 'this little Aesopic sort of an Animal in his own cropt Hair, and Dress agreeable to the Forest he came from'. Gildon's treatment of *Crusoe* was almost as rough but more humorous:

> SCENE, *A great field betwixt* Newington-Green *and* Newington Town, *at one a clock in a Moon-light Morning.*

CRUSOE

Enter D....F...*with two Pocket Pistols.*

D—l. A Fine, pleasurable Morning, I believe about one a Clock; and, I suppose, all the Lazy Kidnapping Rogues are by this Time got drunk with *Geneva* or Malt-Spirits to Bed, and I may pass Home without farther Terror . . . Bless my Eye-Sight, what's this I see! . . . Gentlemen, what would you have? Would you murder me? Take what I have and save my Life.

Cru. Why, Father D...n, dost thou not know thy own Children? Art though so frighted at Devils of thy own raising? I am thy *Robinson Crusoe*, and that, My Man *Friday.*

D...l, Ah! Poor Crusoe, how come you hither? What do you do here?

Cru. Ho, ho, do you know me now? You are like the Devil in *Milton,* that could not tell the offspring of his own Brain, *Sin and Death,* till *Madam Sin* discover'd to them who they were. Yes, it is *Crusoe* and his Man *Friday*, who are come to punish thee now, for making us such Scoundrels in thy Writing: Come Friday, make ready, but don't shoot til I give the Word.

Fri. No shoot, Master, no shoot: me will show how we use Scribblers in my Country . . .

D...l. Hum, hum . . . well, and what are your complaints of me?

Cru. Why, that you have made me a strange whimsical, inconsistent Being, in three Weeks losing all the Religion of a Pious

Education; and when you bring me again to a Sense of the Want of Religion, you make me quit that upon every Whimsy; you make me extravagantly Zealous, and as extravagantly Remiss; you make me an Enemy to all *English* Sailors, and a Panegyrist upon all other Sailors that come in your way: Thus, all the *English* Seamen laugh'd me out of Religion, but the *Spanish* and *Portuguese* Sailors were honest religious Fellows; you make me a Protestant in *London* and a *Papist* in Brasil . . . nor can I forgive you the making me such a Whimsical Dog, to ramble over three Parts of the World after I was sixty-five. Therefore, I say, *Friday*, prepare to shoot.

Fri. No shoot yet Master, me have something to say, he much Injure me too.

D...l. Injure you too, how the Devil have I injur'd you?

Fri. Have injure me, to make me such Blockhead, so much contradiction, as to be able to speak *English tolerably well* in a Month or two, and not to speak it better in twelve Years after; to make me go out to be kill'd by the Savages only to be a Spokesman to them, tho' I did not know, whether they understood one Word of my Language; for you must know, Father *D...n*, that almost ev'ry Nation of us *Indians* speak a different Language. Now Master shall me shoot?

Crusoe holds Friday back so that Defoe can hear the objections of a range of his characters from Volumes I and II, published a mere six weeks before

Gildon's pamphlet hit the streets. The invective—fierce enough to influence Defoe's opening for *Crusoe III*—scarcely eases up at the end of the mock-encounter because Gildon, a sometime successful playwright and, dismayed with the fast onset of blindness, evidently felt that his target's whole politico-literary profile deserved a slapstick finale:

> *D...l.* Common; I hate all that's common, even to common Sense—but no Interruptions Son *Crusoe*, no Interruptions; from thence I may take a Jaunt to the *Greek* Church, in a sort of whimsical *Caravan*, over the Desarts, which I made you pass, if by the way I don't happen to catch a Tartar, that is to take a Leap into the Dark . . .

> *Cru.* Enough, Enough, Father D...n, you have confest enough, and now prepare for your Punishment, for here come all the rest of our Number, which we expected; come *Friday*, pull out the Books, you have both Volumes, have you not *Friday*?

> *Fri.* Yes Master, and me will make him swallow his own Vomit.

> *Cru.* Here, Gentlemen, every one hold a Limb of him.

> *D...l.* Oh, Oh, Mercy! Mercy!

> *Fri.* Swallow, swallow, Father *D...n*, your Writings be good for the Heartburn, swallow, Father *D...n*—so me have cram'd down one volume, must he have the other now Master?

Cru., Yes, yes, Friday, or else the Dose will not be compleat, and so perhaps mayn't work and pass thro' him kindly.

Fri. Come, Father *D...n*, t'other Pill, or I think I may call it Bolus for the bigness of it, it is good for your Health; come if you will make such large Compositions, you must take them for your Pains.

D...l. Oh, oh, oh, oh.

Cru. Now, gentlemen, each Man take his Part of the Blanket and toss him immoderately; for you must know, Gentlemen, that this is the sort of Physick which never works well without a violent Motion. [*They toss him lustily, he crying out all the while.*]

Cru. Hold, Gentlemen, I think our Business is done; for by the unsavoury Stench which assaults my Nostrils, I find the Dose is past thro' him, and so good Morrow, Father *D...n*.

Over the next 48 pages Gildon changes rhetorical approach completely in *An Epistle to D..... D' F...e, The Reputed Author of ROBINSON CRUSOE*. The hectoring and often pedantic objections both to the composition and the doctrinal presumptions of both volumes were pretty standard fare by the polemical customs of the day, and Defoe, of course, was an accomplished proponent himself, as when he attacked Gildon's previous bookseller/publisher Curll:

He is odious in his person, scandalous in his Fame, he is mark'd by Nature, for he has a bawdy Countenace, and a debauched Mien, his Tongue is an Echo of all the beastly Language his Shop is fill'd with, and Filthiness drivels in the very Tone of his Voice.[21]

Still, Gildon probably provided Defoe with the most robust repudiation of *Crusoe* for the next three hundred years, and if Defoe was spared some of the lamer critiques over that time, so was he denied in the final dozen years of his life almost all of the celebrations of his first true fiction.

Gildon's repudiation may have been the most robust, but *Gulliver's Travels* was far more consequential. Deploying only a light parody on *Crusoe*, it delivered a completely excoriating one on the human condition as a whole. We have no record that Jonathan Swift, seven years the younger, ever met Daniel Defoe, although they both wrote journalism in favour of the Harley administration of 1710–1714. We don't know what they thought of each other's greatest book, and there is no mention of *Crusoe* in the list of Swift's books at his death, but he was an avid reader rather than a zealous collector. Swift, the socially superior, Anglican Tory priest devoted as much to scatological shock as classical quotation, never mentioned Defoe by name in any written record that has come down to us. But the references—suitably snide and deliberately diminishing—are there. In 1708, Swift took a pretty open shot at Defoe's *Review:*

. . . however insipid soever those papers are, they seemed to be levelled to the understanding of a great number; they are grown a necessary part of coffee-house furniture . . . One of these authors (the fellow that was pilloried I have forgot his name) is indeed so grave, sententious, dogmatical a rogue that there is no enduring him . . .[22]

Defoe had earlier been prompted to pen his chaotic and thinly parodic lunar travel tale *The Consolidator* by Swift's artful and immensely popular promotion of Anglican moderation in *A Tale of a Tub*. Perhaps he did not then appreciate whom he was up against, but by 1710 there was no doubt that Swift disliked as well as despised Defoe, who indeed waxed sententious as well as pedantic when described (alongside the editor of the *Observator*) as one of a pair of

> stupid, illiterate Scribblers, both of them *Fanaticks* by Profession . . . the mock authoritative Manner of the one, and the insipid Mirth of the other, however insupportable to reasonable Ears, being of a Level with a great Numbers amongst the lowest part of Mankind.[23]

That seems to be the last direct tirade from Swift, but in 1726, when it was long clear that these two authors had staked out different notions of humanity as well as political preference and expressive style, Defoe returned to the fray with the author of the Yahoos and Houyhnhnms in his discussion of Peter, the 'Wild Boy of Hamelin', who had aroused similar debate over the reasoning, animalistic qualities and moral stature of *Homo sapiens*. In his reflective pamphlet *Mere Nature Delineated*, Defoe shows that he has not forgotten the earlier exchanges even as he engages in unusual, 'Swiftian' passages of blunt physicality. It is hard to read this text as a precise rejoinder to *Gulliver*, but it certainly takes aim at Swift:

> If [my serious vein of thought] should be disagreeable to the fashionable Levity of the Times on that Account, some that have more Wit than I, may turn it into a Jest, and Burlesque the Calamity of Mankind, if they think it more agreeable: I am mighty willing to leave it to the learned Dr S-; for he that can Preach and read Prayers in the Morning, write Baudy in the Afternoon, banter Heaven and Religion, and write prophanely at Night; and then read Prayers and Preach again the next Morning, and so on in a due Rotation of Extremes; is much fitter than I am for turning the Tears of the Unhappy into a Ballad, and making a Mock of human Misery.[24]

It is generally agreed that *Gulliver* is not a 'novel' in the same sense that *Crusoe* internalises providence and reflects anxiously upon the outer world. Swift/ Gulliver move with brisk dispatch through the latter's four voyages, undeterred by direct speech in a satirical sequence through magnitudes (Lilliput and Brobdingnag), the delusions of science (Laputa), and the misanthropic message of Houyhnhnm-equine dominion over the humanoid Yahoos. Perhaps Defoe was annoyed by the resolute secularism of a text written by a man many years before ordained into the Church and now Dean of St. Patrick's in Dublin?[25] Maybe he felt that the early reference in *Gulliver* to 'my cousin Dampier' was an uncoded fingering of one of his core sources? He could not have failed to see that Gulliver, like Crusoe, was a third son with an uncontainable desire to go to sea. A shipwreck opens Swift's first voyage tale and a mutiny his fourth, out of which Gulliver escapes in a canoe. Portuguese captains provide assistance to both travellers.[26]

We know that Swift began drafting *Gulliver* shortly after the publication of *Crusoe*, so he evidently had all three volumes to eye. But the light plagiarising of scenes and circumstances would already have been familiar to Defoe, who was from the off up against publishing pirates as well as those on the high seas. What must have been deeply offensive, however, was the deployment of these familiar narrative devices to the end of stripping bare a civilisation that he sought to improve. Swift's infamous 'excremental vision' is never far away—and deployed to ludic effect in the final voyage by the Yahoos, of course, whereas Crusoe never gets lavatorial. Women abound in *Gulliver*, one fancying him when seen naked; Crusoe is almost always fully clothed and, as we have seen, the female presence is minimised to an almost monastic degree. Moreover, as Michael McKeon nicely puts it, Crusoe ends in an 'atmosphere thick with fair dealing', while Gulliver returns home to dine with his wife and 'find the Smell of a Yahoo continuing very offensive, I always keep my Nose well stopt with Rue, Lavender, or Tobacco-Leaves'.[27] Although it was distinctly 'after the fact', even the bowdlerisation of both books into child-friendly abridgements might be said to follow polarised paths with Crusoe a kind of meccano-building hero, and Gulliver prone to naughty words even as he labours against the little people and then the big ones. We do not know what the authors really thought because those quoted above are Defoe's last reported words on the matter, and there is no record that Swift ever deigned to take it up over the years up to his death in 1745.

Nothing since—either in an original text or in its surreptitious social-isation-through-infantilisation—has come remotely close to *Gulliver* as a response to *Crusoe*, despite the fact that Swift merely skimmed off a few motifs at the service of a satire on human pride rather than a celebration of man's resilience. *Gulliver* may fairly be said to stand readily on its own, but that is scarcely less true of some other texts and authors for whom Defoe had offered an example, reference, or inspiration.

*

The true projection of *Crusoe* into an effective element of world liter-ature took place in two stages late in the eighteenth century. First, with a simple clarion call of admiration by Jean-Jacques Rousseau in his trea-tise-novel *Émile* (1762) and then, directly motivated by Rousseau, through the supremely well-organised abridgement *Robinson der Jungere* (1779–80) by Joachim Henrich Campe, who may be dubbed the founding father of the *Robinsonaden*/'Robinsonade' tradition that, rapidly retailing in French and English (*Robinson the Younger,* 1789), set off the parallax version beloved of children and teachers of every stripe seeking a handy isolated human being capable of calculus. Tellingly, both versions focus almost exclusively on the island experience.

Rousseau's book is with us despite the worst efforts of the Paris *Parlement* and the stern Calvinists who ran Geneva, both of which deemed *Émile* as well as the author's *Contrat social*—published a few months earlier, and noting that 'Adam was sovereign over the world, like Crusoe on his island, for so long as he was the sole inhabitant'—to be dangerous texts. Rousseau was able to do a runner, but his books were burned as 'rash, scandalous, impious, tending to destroy the Christian religion and all governments'.[28] As Rousseau's work was prone to do, a treatise, effectively on moral philosophy but notionally on the best manner in which a child might be educated, morphed in the final third into a love story, but neither that nor the passages on *Crusoe*—which, as we have seen, was already widely available in translation—offended the censors. For, despite the fact that he was helping the promotion of a free-thinking and rationally calculating model, Rousseau valued Crusoe overwhelmingly for his experience of nature and his response to it.

Rousseau, something of a failed tutor, lingers the better part of 150 pages before, embedded in Book III, he lets slip that,

> I hate books; they only teach us about things we know nothing about . . . Is there no way of correlating so many lessons scattered through so many books, no way of focussing them on some common object, easy to see, interesting to follow, and stimulating even to a child?

There is; but we must still wait a while,

> Eager philosopher, I see your imagination at work. Spare yourself the trouble; this state is already known, it is described with due respect to you, far better than you could describe it, at least with

greater truth and simplicity. Since we must have books, there is one book which, to my thinking, supplies the best treatise on an education according to nature. This is the first book Émile will read; for a long time it will form his whole library, and it will always retain an honoured place . . . What is this wonderful book? Is it Aristotle? Pliny? Buffon? No; it is *Robinson Crusoe*.

Rousseau then outlines the essence of the book's appeal as succinctly as any since:

Robinson Crusoe on his island, deprived of the help of his fellow-men, without the means of carrying on the various arts, yet finding food, preserving his life, and procuring certain amount of comfort; this is the thing to interest people of all ages, and it can be made attractive to children in all sorts of ways. We shall thus make a reality of that desert island which formerly served as an illustration. The condition, I confess, is not that of a social being, nor is it in all probability Émile's own condition, but he should use it as a standard of comparison for all other conditions. The surest way to raise him above prejudice and to base his judgements on the true relation of things, is to put him in the place of a solitary man, and to judge all things as they would be judged by such a man in relation to their own utility.[29]

Rousseau then strips the novel 'of irrelevant matter', which is to say everything before and after the island experience in making his condensed Enlightenment appropriation of Defoe's tale. But his contribution is really just a slogan; he never proceeds to make the apparently easy translation from adult illustration to child-friendly reality. That piece of literary heavy lifting was undertaken by Campe, who intuited that he needed not just to provide an expurgated story but also to do so in the format of it being told to children. Accordingly, *Robinson the Younger* comes in thirty-one evening-sized sections and is delivered with all the dramatic timing and explanatory asides of a truly proficient tutor. (After all, Campe had taught Wilhelm and Alexander von Humboldt, who were demanding pupils in very different ways.)

The Campe version is not a total travesty—to remove the Crusoe family from Hull to Exeter or replace the goats with llamas could, even from the vantage point of Braunschweig, be deemed a neat and harmless sleight of editorial hand. However, it does dispense with all but the most basic elements of the pre-island experience, the removal of articles from the wreck (so, no guns for a good while), and the prolonged scenes with the mutineers/pirates. Friday—who is saved with the use of a spear—is introduced on page 95 (fifteenth evening) of the 183 that constitute the 1782 English edition.

Campe's English translators assign the duties of bedtime narration to Mr. Billingsley, who addresses a quietly substantial group of his wife, friends Mr. Rose and Mr. Meredith (very marginal roles), and the successively introduced children—Harriet, Edward (very chirpy), Charlotte, Henry, George, and Richard—who raise queries pertinent to their age and opine with an assurance true to all. The resulting text is certainly not that imagined by Rousseau, and one soon encounters enough piety to please the authorities in Paris and Geneva as well as some reassuring stereotypes, as when Richard asks why Crusoe alone had been spared in the shipwreck:

Mr. Bill. Have you not learnt long ago, that God knows all things better than we poor mortals do? Since, therefore, God loves all mankind as his children, it is impossible but he should do what is best for our interest.

Geo. Without doubt.

Mr. Bill. Well, my dear Richard, do you wish now to repeat the question you asked me just now?

Rich. What question?

Mr. Bill. Why the Supreme Disposer of things saved only Robinson Crusoe, and suffered the rest to perish? Probably Robinson's life was preserved to the end that affliction might be a school of wisdom to him.

Keep this in remembrance, my dear child; and instead of rashly endeavouring to reason or explain the seeming inconsistency, say to yourself, 'God knows better than I what is for my good. I am convinced that his dispensations of good and evil are ever intended to render us better than we are'.

Henry. Did Robinson think so upon that occasion?

Mr. Bill. Yes, and praying to God for pardon, resolved to amend his life—When the joy that he felt on his happy deliverance had subsided, he looked about him, but could not perceive, on any side, the least mark that the country was inhabited.

This was a dreadful necessity imposed on him. But his anxiety was still more dreadfully increased when this reflection occurred to him, 'What if there should be wild beasts or savages here, so that I might not be able to live in safety!'

Charlotte. What are savages, papa?

Rich. Savages are wild men. Have you never heard talk of them, Charlotte? In countries, a great, great way off from this, there are men nearly as wild as beasts.

Charlotte. Do they ever come here?

Mr. Bill. No, the countries where these unfortunate people live are so far off that they never come here.[30]

By the twenty-fourth evening we have reached a kind of convergence with the original, passing through the footprint, the demanding moment when Friday wants to disinter the two cannibals killed in his liberation so that they can be eaten, and demonstration of the power of firearms, but, by dint of skipping the pre-island scenes, we have evaded the issue of slavery. Here the passage of time from a text written within five years of formal British control of the international slave trade begins to show through:

Henry. Traffic for slaves, papa?

Mr. Bill. I will explain it to you.

In Africa, which is the country of the negroes, men, in igno-
rance and stupidity, do not seem to differ much from the brutes.
Their chiefs or kings, who are as savage as themselves, treat them
accordingly. If any Europeans arrive on their coast, whole crowds
of blacks are offered to them for sale as we sell cattle here in a
market. Even fathers bring their children, and exchange them for
trifles. Thus the Europeans every year purchase a great number of
negroes, and carry them to the West Indies, where they are forced
to work at the hardest labour.

Rich. It is not well done to use human beings in that manner.

Mr. Bill. Certainly it is very unjust; and we have hopes that in time
this iniquitous traffic of slaves will be abolished.[31]

The contrivance of a happy ending requires some further adjustment,
including the return of Robinson and Friday to Exeter, where Crusoe senior not only survived but wished his son to succeed him as a broker.

. . . but Robinson, long accustomed to the pleasure of manual
labour, begged his permission to learn the trade of a carpenter, and his father not opposing his inclination, he put himself,
together with Friday, apprentice to that business, in which they
made such proficiency, that, before the end of the year, they could
work with as much neatness and dispatch as any of the trade in
Exeter . . . Concord between themselves, indulgence for the faults
of others, beneficence towards those they knew, and humanity

to all men were virtues so habitual to them, that they could not conceive how any one who neglected the practice of them could be happy . . .

Here Mr Billingsley was silent; the children continued sitting some little time longer, in deep reflection, until this thought, I will endeavour to do the same, which resulted as a moral from what they had heard, took root in the breath of each, and acquired the force of an immoveable resolution.[32]

Perhaps it was just as well that Rousseau had been dead for over a decade when Campe's pietistic response to his eulogy hit the bookshops. Yet, if it engendered the *Robinsonade* tradition—most particularly in the doubly domesticated *Der Schweizerische Robinson* (1812) by Johann David Wyss—that in itself did not remove the original from continued reassessment.

Indeed, as Pat Rogers noted long ago, 'Strangely—as some might think—it was the Romantic movement which lifted prosaic old Daniel Defoe, controversialist and compiler, to the status of a major artist'.[33] Coleridge, whose *Rime of the Ancient Mariner*, drew on maritime sources close to those used by Defoe, was nowhere more admiring than in his annotations in the margins of *Crusoe*:

I smil'd to my self at the sight of this money, O drug! Said I aloud, what art thou good for? Thou art not worth to me, no not the taking off of the ground, one of those knives is worth all this heap . . . However, upon second thoughts I took it away. (47)

To which Coleridge responds:

> Worthy of Shakespeare; and yet the simple semi-colon after it, the
> instant pressing on without the least pause of reflex consciousness
> is more exquisite and masterlike than the touch itself. A meaner
> writer, a Marmontel, would have put an '!' after 'away', and com-
> menced a new paragraph.[34]

For Walter Scott all the fuss about the empirical origins of *Crusoe* paled in
comparison to the transformative skills of Defoe's prose:

> The assistance which De Foe received from Selkirk's history,
> seems of a very meagre kind . . . [He] borrowed, perhaps, from
> the account of Woodes Rogers, the circumstance of the two huts,
> the abundance of goats, the clothing made out of their skin; and
> the turnips of Alexander Selkirk may have perhaps suggested the
> corn of Robinson Crusoe. Even these incidents, however, are so
> wrought up and heightened, and so much is added to make them
> interesting, that the bare circumstances occurring elsewhere, can-
> not be said to infringe upon the author's claim to originality.[35]

Two generations later, at the outset of *The Moonstone*, Wilkie Collins gushes
like a trueborn fan:

> I am not superstitious; I have read a heap of books in my time;
> I am a scholar in my own way. Though turned seventy, I possess
> an active memory, and legs to correspond. You are not to take it,

if you please, as the saying of an ignorant man, when I express my opinion that such a book as *Robinson Crusoe* never was written, and never will be written again. I have tried that book for years—generally in combination with a pipe of tobacco—and I have found it my friend in need in all the necessities of this mortal life. When my spirits are bad—*Robinson Crusoe*. In past times when my wife plagued me; in present times when I have had a drop too much—*Robinson Crusoe*. I have worn out six stout *Robinson Crusoes* with hard work in my service. On my lady's last birthday she gave me a seventh. I took a drop too much on the strength of it; and *Robinson Crusoe* put me right again. Price four shillings and sixpence, bound in blue, with pictures into the bargain.[36]

The enthusiasm was not universal. In the same year Leslie Stephen displayed what Rogers calls 'an Arnoldian capacity for dismissal':

De Foe, even in *Robinson Crusoe*, gives a very inadequate picture of the mental torments to which his hero is exposed. He is frightened by a parrot calling him by name, and by the strangely picturesque incident of the footmark on the sand; but, on the whole, he takes his imprisonment with preternatural stolidity. His stay on the island produces the same state of mind as might be due to a dull Sunday in Scotland. For this reason, the want of power in describing emotion as compared with the amazing power of describing facts, *Robinson Crusoe* is a book for boys rather than men, and, as Lamb says, for the kitchen rather than higher circles. It falls short of any high intellectual interest . . .[37]

This Swiftian disdain was not, however, shared by the likes of George Borrow, Jules Verne, Robert Louis Stevenson, James Joyce, or, indeed, Stephen's own daughter, Virginia Woolf. But there is nowhere quite like the university in which to argue over the book and its status.

The Rise of the Novel and Its Critics

Ian Watt (1917–1999) was a most unusual academic. Born in Westmoreland, educated in Dover and St. John's College, Cambridge, he was wounded in the Battle for Singapore in February 1942, and spent the rest of World War II as a prisoner of war of the Japanese, working on the Burma Railway, where he became very ill but narrowly avoided succumbing, unlike twelve thousand others. As he later commented, Watt and his comrades had to learn to become prisoners—'being a prisoner is not an easy task'.[38] Perhaps this gave him greater sympathy to Crusoe's position than could be summoned by Leslie Stephen? What it certainly provided was a fineness of human touch enabling him to navigate with grace and learning a wholesale academic controversy in which the objective of many was precisely to take no prisoners at all:

> [Watt] made some really big mistakes—he thought there was a 'novel'; he thought that it had a beginning; he assumed it was a narrative fiction that displaced previous narrative fictions and had a 'rise' located in metropole England. In doing so, he was

naïve, sexist, racist, Anglophilic, logocentric, essentialist, positiv-
ist, vulgarly materialist, and probably homophobic. But nobody
is perfect.[39]

Luckily, Lennard Davis is here in jest, but we do have at least to tiptoe
around the headlines of some very serious critical disputation over a topic
at the heart of literary study.

Although he was almost always writing, Watt was also an inveterate
editor of his work, and, together with a long delayed study of Conrad, his
core contribution to the study of literature can be identified in three titles:
'Robinson Crusoe as a Myth' (1951); *The Rise of the Novel: Studies in Defoe,
Richardson and Fielding* (1957); and *Myths of Modern Individualism: Faust, Don
Quixote, Don Juan, Robinson Crusoe* (1996). As can be discerned from the titles
there is a common—if evolving—interpretative thread through this cor-
pus, which reflects the uncommon influence not just of wartime captiv-
ity, which had interrupted his Cambridge Ph.D. (*The Novel and its Reader,
1719–1754*) and yielded the paltry compensation of £76.10.0, but also those
of Theodor Adorno, whom Watt met during a fellowship at UCLA, and
Talcott Parsons, likewise at Harvard. In its inception British—it would
often be denounced as 'empiricist' and never quite lost the imprint of F.
R. Leavis—Watt's thesis always possessed an American directness, which
was not diminished after he took up a post at Stanford University in 1964.

From the start Watt was anxious not to see *Crusoe* as simply a text, or
even as a text amongst other texts. In linking it to *Faust, Don Juan*, and *Don
Quixote*, he identified it as a myth, as understood by Malinowski:

It is not in the nature of fiction, such as we read today in a novel, but it is a living reality, believed to have happened in primitive times, and continuing ever since to influence the world and human destinies.[40]

He then picks out the feature that most appealed to Rousseau—radical individualism—but insists against Rousseau that the book is 'fundamentally anti-primitivist' and that Defoe's essential concern is with labour as 'part of the ideology of a new and vast historical process'.

Defoe's readers . . . rejoice to find that isolation can be the beginning of a realization of the potentialities of the individual. Their inertias are cheered by a vicarious participation in Crusoe's twenty-three [sic] years of lonely and triumphant struggle.[41]

Reflecting the input of Talcott Parsons, Watt intertwines Max Weber with more predictable literary sources:

Crusoe, in fact, has been stranded in the utopia of the Protestant Ethic. There temptation, whether economic or moral, is wholly absent. Crusoe's energies cannot be deflected, either by the picnic promises of pastoral utopias, or by the relaxing and uneconomic piety of the hermits and mystics who are heroes of an earlier form of Christianity, heroes whose faith is measured by their certainty that 'God will provide'.[42]

That, so to speak, to the left. But Watt is no less concerned to dispatch the alternative Crusoe on the right, 'that lonely and unlovely archetype of our civilisation, *homo economicus*'.

> Homo economicus, is, of course, a fiction. There has long been a conflict about the utility of the abstraction. Briefly, the classical political economists found in the idea of Robinson Crusoe, the solitary individual on a desert island, a splendid example for their system-building. On the other hand, their critics who, like Marx, were concerned to prove that economics can be a guide to reality only when it is a historical and a social science, have denied the relevance of Robinson Crusoe to any realistic economic thinking.[43]

Watt goes a little further, but not much, in this article. The space that he has set up—of a text in history that has real things to say whilst being imagined in both creation and reception—needs a more developed interpretation.

This is provided in *The Rise of the Novel*, which expands the history and deepens the methodology of 'Crusoe as Myth'. Key to this regard is Watt's controversial notion of 'formal realism',

> . . . formal, because the term realism does not here refer to any special literary doctrine or purpose, but only to a set of narrative procedures which are so commonly found together in the novel, and so rarely in other literary genres, that they may be regarded as typical of the form itself . . . that the novel is a full and authentic

report of human experience, and is therefore under an obligation to satisfy its reader with such details of the story as the individuality of the actors concerned, the particulars of the times and places of their actions . . .[44]

If 'realism' is not to become a simple text-bound tautology, it must derive authenticity from outside, from its reception, and that is achieved in *Crusoe* through the specific calibration of its 'individualism':

Defoe, whose philosophical outlook has much in common with that of the English empiricists of the seventeenth century, expressed the diverse elements of individualism more completely than any previous writer.[45]

That very diversity—alien to the neoclassical economists and needing concrete social form for Marx—lay in a transitional moment in English society.

. . . the primacy of the economic motive, and an innate reverence for book-keeping and the law of contract, are by no means the only matters in which Robinson Crusoe is a symbol of processes associated with the rise of economic individualism. The hypostasis of the economic motive logically entails a devaluation of other modes of thought, feeling, and action: the various forms of traditional group relationship, the family, the guild, the village, the sense of nationality—all are weakened, and so, too, are the competing claims of non-economic individual achievement and enjoyment, ranging from spiritual salvation to the pleasures of recreation.[46]

Watt has now managed to apply Weber more precisely—his work would be subject to all the critical consequences of that—and he has also found a means of reconciling his approach with that of Marx, by reaching back beyond *Capital* to the Paris Notebooks of 1844:

> In his blindness to aesthetic experience Crusoe is Defoe's peer. We can say of him as Marx said of his archetypal capitalist: 'enjoyment is subordinated to capital, and the individual who enjoys to the individual who capitalizes'.[47]

But, Watt insists, Crusoe stands at the start of that process—he cannot, of course, enjoy his money on the island—and he still exhibits

> a confusion of religious and material values to which the Puritan gospel of the dignity of labour was peculiarly liable: once the highest spiritual values had been attached to the performance of the daily task, the next step was for the autonomous individual to regard his achievements as a quasi-divine mastering of the environment . . . Economic individualism explains much of Crusoe's character; economic specialization and its associated ideology help to account for the appeal of his adventure; but it is Puritan individualism which controls his spiritual being.[48]

In his final book Watt places *Crusoe* at the end of a series of myths because its hero can alone prosper in the face of the ideational and structural constraints of the Counter-Reformation. In *The Rise of the Novel*, by contrast, Ian Watt depicts the book as opening a trajectory that would reach through Richardson and Fielding through to fulfilment in Jane Austen (that is the Leavis line, but some would argue James Joyce and Virginia Woolf), after which there is nowhere new for 'formal realism' to go.

*

You didn't write this sort of stuff during the Cold War without attracting a response. As Watt himself wryly reflected,

> Reviewing belongs to the large class of benevolent-aggressive dyadic relationships which are characterized, like dentistry, by an extreme asymmetry of roles. The transitive agent, the reviewer, is secure in the knowledge that his sitting duck can neither fly off nor hit back; despite this great freedom, however, reviewers seem to operate under a highly conventional set of institutionalized imperatives, all naturally directed towards producing the most pain with the least effort.[49]

He really shouldn't have worried. As recently as 2010, more than sixty years after its publication, his book was still being objected to—'For all its answers to the big questions about the emergence of the novel, Ian Watt's *The Rise of the Novel* (1957) has seemed increasingly unconvincing in recent years'.[50]

The first wave of objections predictably focused on Watt's materialism, his method—depicted as teleological in its assumption of an historic arc of development of the novel form—and his systematic under-appreciation of the spiritual biography in *Crusoe* as he postulated what Paul Hunter called 'a triple rise'—first of the middle class, then of the reading public, and finally of the novel itself—not one element of which could be given firm historiographical confirmation.[51] Both Hunter and George Starr had more than enough knowledge of late-seventeenth and early-eighteenth century religious literature to make some telling factual as well as analytical points. And in the case of Hunter, one of the main sources for this was one Timothy Cruso.

Timothy Cruso was only five years older than Daniel Defoe, and he attended the same school, Charles Morton's academy in Newington Green. Cruso was a skilled and influential Presbyterian preacher whose sermons were published regularly from 1690 onwards. We should take him seriously, even if he died in 1697, more than twenty years before publication of the book that bears a version of his name. For Hunter, Cruso's admonitions from the pulpit cannot be elbowed aside by sociological generalisation, because '*Robinson Crusoe* is structured on the basis of a familiar Christian pattern of disobedience-punishment-repentence-deliverance, a pattern set up in the first few pages of the book.'[52]

Watt had got it wrong—the spiritual isn't the subordinate, vestigial element; it is at least an equal driver, and arguably more important still:

> Throughout *Robinson Crusoe* physical events affect Crusoe's
> spiritual state, for Crusoe is concerned with accommodating
> himself to his world spiritually and physically at the same time,
> and his efforts to come to terms with his physical environment
> parallel his efforts to find a proper relationship with his God.
> Ultimately, his physical activities become a metaphor for his
> spiritual aspirations.[53]

Crusoe, then, isn't 'realist' in making fiction seem like fact; it is not a psy-
cho-travel drama for comfortably domesticated English readers; and it is
not a parable on political economy. Elements of all these may be found, but
the dominant feature is Defoe's development of 'Puritan thought patterns
and . . . rich subliterary context'.

To drive this home, Hunter properly reminds us of the power of the
sermon, which had by the mid-twentieth century not just waned in influence in the Christian world but also lost almost all recognition of its erst-
while predominance over the press. Here is Timothy Cruso preaching at
Crutched Friars in 1695:

> The days wherein we live are extremely Evil, but yet we have
> a sad and doleful Prospect of the next Age becoming worse, if
> God do not by some effectual means stop the Wicked Course
> of the Rising Generation. We see such Crouds and Swarms of
> young Ones continually posting down to Hell, and bringing up so
> much of Hell in the midst of us, that both in compassion to them
> and to our Native Countrey, we cannot but use some Christian

Vera Effigies
TIMOTHEI CRUSO.
Ætat. 40. 1697.

Timothy Cruso by Robert White, after Thomas Forster.
© National Portrait Gallery, London.

endeavors to open the Eyes of these Mad Prodigals, and to fetch them home.

These motifs are undeniably scattered throughout the novel, albeit in worried, reflexive, and self-admonitory register. So too is a version of Timothy Cruso's injunction, 'You who would make a safe and prosperous Voyage over *this deep and wide Sea of Temptations* ought to be well-fortified against the tempter at your *first setting out*'.[54]

For Pat Rogers, the piling up of sermons is actually no more convincing than the generalisations of historical sociology if too many exclusionary claims are based upon it. Hunter over-claimed in 'using standard metaphors, parables and symbols to create a moral pilgrimage rather than a bare escape story'. That, however, was in the mid-1960s, and just as Watt had broken with the narrow aridity of textual exegesis, so had the 'religious revisionists' now provided a corrective to his historicism.[55]

But, of course, Daniel Defoe did not live in the twentieth century. For him, as for Timothy Cruso, the real danger in the 1690s—apart from Jacobite restoration of Catholicism—was precisely the deism trading surreptitiously behind 'common sense'. Here is Defoe in a splendidly unreasonable voice nearly a decade after writing *Crusoe*:

The problem is that the Deists want a God who is limited in his power; a God without a Devil, according to Epicurus; a God Wise and Powerful, but not infinitely so, not Ominpotent, not Self-Sufficient, and All-sufficient; a God that having created the World (and 'tis with some difficulty they go so far) has not the power to guide it, but has abandoned it to the Government of it self; to that foolish Nothing, that unexisting place of Nonsense, call'd Chance; or like the Followers of Zeno, the Deist Philosopher, a God depending upon (they know not what of a) blind Destiny; a God who not being able to break the Chain of second Causes, is carry'd away with them himself, being obliged to act by the Course of natural Consequences, even whether he will or no.[56]

Defoe, after all, wrote *The Political History of the Devil* in more than satirical mode, and in the year that *Crusoe* appeared George I was obliged to veto a bill in the Irish Parliament that would have punished unregistered Catholic priests with castration.[57] We may wish to agree with John Richetti that 'Defoe's . . . work expresses a consistent mixture of secular modernity, with all that implies about human agency and autonomy, and an apparently sincere religious conviction', but any such *via media* was far from stable and moved mercurially between some quite distant poles. As we will see, Defoe would go to jail several times for the expression of wildly intemperate views, sometimes in parody of those who opposed his beliefs.

*

Karl Marx's attitude to this whole issue was engagingly direct: 'Of his prayers and the like, we take no account, since our friend takes pleasure in them and sees them as recreation'.[58] Ian Watt thinks this goes too far, and it could well be that the academic debate over the relative materialist and religious motifs in *Crusoe* has distracted us from other codes within the text as well as themes omitted from it.

CRUSOE

Tom Paulin definitely thinks so, arguing that the chronology of the narrative has an allegorical relevance to the politics of the Stuart Restoration and, most particularly, of the suppression of the Duke of Monmouth's rising in 1685. For Paulin, Timothy Cruso is important less for his Presbyterian preaching than because Defoe refers to him in the company of the 'Western martyrs' from Morton's Newington Green Academy at and after the Battle of Sedgemoor (6 July 1685). We have no direct source that places Daniel Defoe at the battle, but we do have documentary evidence that he was subsequently pardoned (31 May 1687) for his involvement in the uprising.

Paulin—a fine poet of Presbyterian background—wants us to focus on words such as 'hurry', which in the eighteenth century, and particularly in Ireland, carried the strong connotation of social and political disturbance as well as speed. We can easily skim over such potent inferences (others, of more Freudian inclination, may want us to reconfigure 'fence'). For Paulin, Defoe exhibits 'survivor's guilt' in *Crusoe*, mentioning six times the date 30 September 1659—it is, after all, the day he landed on the island. It may, of course, also be Defoe's birthday (of which we have no record), but it was certainly the day in 1685 on which Benjamin Hewling, twenty-two and a former fellow pupil at Stoke Newington, was hanged at Lyme Regis under Judge Jeffreys's Bloody Assizes. Hewling's younger brother, William, had been hanged a fortnight earlier. Tom Paulin feels that the memory of such losses may very well have influenced the description of Crusoe's miraculous escape from the shipwreck. Certainly the sad memory would have been freshened by the publication in 1705 of *The Western Martyrology* by John Tutchin, then rivalling Defoe as a pamphleteer but twenty years earlier a rebel condemned by Jeffreys to be whipped through every market town in Dorset once a year for seven years. Perhaps unsurprisingly a legend developed that Tutchin 'petitioned James II to be hanged instead, but neither sentence was carried out'.[59]

Ian Watt didn't like to use the term 'bourgeois' since he felt that it carried all the cargo of a historical theory girded on metaphysics, but for Tom Paulin, always with one figurative foot outside the academy,

> Defoe is the prose laureate of classic bourgeois revolution, and in the chaos of Crusoe's landfall he is representing that revolution, rather as Blok seeks to give images of the Russian Revolution in 'The Twelve'.[60]

Of course, you can buy the salience of 30 September without purchasing the Bourgeois Revolution on the fly, and it is always good to be reminded of what might be hidden in plain sight.

In this regard, opinion seems pretty divided over whether Defoe efficiently expunged sex from his tale or whether, despite all his primness, he was unable to suppress at least some coded references, evident to contemporary readers who could multi-valorise 'hurry' or visible to analysts of our own day ever ready to spot the libido in drag. Here Ian Watt makes a calm observation across the ages:

> Crusoe's attitude to women is also marked by an extreme inhibition of what we now consider to be normal human feelings. There are, of course, none on the island, and their absence is not

deplored. When Crusoe does notice the lack of 'society', he prays for company, but it is for that of a male slave. With Friday, he is fully satisfied by an idyll without benefit of woman. It is an interesting break from the traditional expectations aroused by desert islands, from the *Odyssey* to the *New Yorker*.[61]

Crusoe makes no bones about the fact that 'I was removed from all the Wickedness of the World here' . . . no lusts (102). But for those who can hunt down metaphors, 'reinscription' might be found in the spilling of the seed, the proliferating female cats, or a homoerotic displacement with Friday.[62] None the less, it is surely germane to the story's easy abridgement that there is no overt hint at masturbation—still less Selkirk-like congress with goats—which would have caused 'the text to tumble backward into . . . the filthy mire of the material'.[63] There is nothing to touch the erotics of Aphra Behn or Eliza Haywood; none of the serial fornication in Neville's *The Isle of Pines*, or even of the allusiveness in *Moll Flanders* and *Roxana*. Defoe's plot in *Crusoe* enables him to avoid the circumlocution that John Richetti sees as the suggestive limit of the later *Conjugal Lewdness*:

> As I am speaking to the married Persons only, in this Part. I need explain my self no farther than to say, there are Bounds and Measures, Times and Seasons, which Nature and Decency always will dictate to them, and will regulate too, and teach them to regulate between themselves their most intimate conjugal Delights and Embraces.[64]

The other great and conspicuous absence—at least at the start of the story—is that of any human beyond Crusoe dwelling on an island that, as Peter Hulme reminds us, would have been populated long before if it could in physical terms possibly be inhabited.[65] This 'magical extraction', in the words of Raymond Williams, is the *sine qua non* of the tale's epic qualities, whether they are based on solitude or industry.[66] It is also, however, central to a reading of the colonial, Caribbean, and civilisational qualities of the text and its context. For Hulme, 'the "spiritual" reading of *Robinson Crusoe* attempts—unsuccessfully—to remedy the scandal of the secular text whose interpretation is not guided by any authorial voice'. Crusoe certainly represents a form of radical individualism, but in the same sense as Descartes's self-conscious subjectivity. Defoe's creation is one which

> Staggers backwards into the future, lacking in self-understanding, full of guilt, self-contradictory, fearful, violent: the modernity of European consciousness shipwrecked in the Caribbean, that very archipelago of its subversion.[67]

Perhaps this is to read too much of the future—revolutions in Haiti and Cuba—back into Defoe's time, but Hulme is surely right to insist that the book's complexity extends to the depiction of slavery, which, in the shape of Friday, is presented as volunteered and rewarded with armament, scarcely in keeping with the historical record. On the other hand, Crusoe's whole island sojourn results from the failure of a voyage designed to trade slaves—something Gildon was quick to accuse Defoe of promoting. A sophisticated argument can be made that in the story Friday conferred

upon Crusoe the right to treat him as a servant.[68] However, in 'real life'
Daniel Defoe was apparently quite clear about the material conditions in
the sugar islands of the Caribbean that 'naturalised' this form of bondage:

> The work of the islands, which is the planting of canes, and
> making sugar, whether in the field or in the sugar-works, is of
> that nature, the labour so severe, the climate so hot, the food
> so course, that no Europeans were ever yet found that could go
> thro' it—At least to the profit of the planter—they must have
> people us'd to the extremities of the weather, entirely subjected
> to the government and correction of the cruellest masters; that
> they may be whip'd forward like horses, can live on what is next
> to the offal of food, like beasts, and never knew better; that have
> the strength of the ox, and knew no more of liberty; and that suf-
> fer every thing the horse suffered, but being flead when they are
> dead, which would be done too, if they could get 6d for the hide.[69]

Here Defoe may well be parodying the views of others, as he often did in
the *Review*. But he also used his columns there to promote trade in a manner
to suggest that a serious purpose underpinned any exaggeration:

> I divide the care and concern of the nation among these gener-
> als, religion, constitution and commerce. Trade I rank in hand
> with religion and constitution . . . improving and extending our
> colonies and trade in America, Africa and Muscovy, in order
> to increase the consumption of our manufactures, and secure

an employ to our people, let the accidents of war be what they will . . .[70]

Five years later he was succinct to the point of bluntness:

> The case is as plain as cause and consequence: Mark the climax.
> No African trade, no negroes; no negroes, no sugars, gingers,
> indicoes etc; no sugars etc no islands; no islands no continent; no
> continent no trade . . .[71]

Here, with the monopoly on the slave trade removed in 1698 from the Royal African Company, Defoe was spelling out to his readership the consequences he feared would ensue by the 'Separate Traders' swamping the market. But, of course, those fears were entirely unjustified, not least because under the Treaty of Utrecht the British were granted the *asiento*, an exclusive licence to import up to forty-eight hundred African slaves a year into the Spanish Caribbean for thirty years.

Homo Economicus Redux

In his first publication on *Crusoe* Ian Watt crisply declared Homo economicus 'a fiction'. Some seventy years later Matthew Watson has shown just how alive that fiction has remained, most notably in those putative enclaves of 'facts'—economic textbooks:

> Neoclassical economics is utterly reliant for the coherence of its
> pedagogical structure on the self-serving appropriation of the

original story of Defoe's shipwrecked sailor. The purpose of turning him from one example of economic man to another is to allow for the creation of readily solvable questions of allocative efficiency.[72]

This appropriation of a 'Robinson Crusoe Economy' has mostly been at the service of illustrating the 'marginalism' at the heart of neoclassical economics although, as Watson notes, they are teaching aids 'that inspire students analytically to think of markets as pristine economic institutions'.[73]

Within that wider imagery, neoclassical economists' concern with microeconomic decision-making perhaps naturally led them to engage with Crusoe more readily than had the classical economists such as Smith and Ricardo, who were not principally concerned with understanding or depicting individual decision-making. For Watson, the more accurate genealogy would be through Rousseau's mythic appropriation of Crusoe and then Campe's popularisation that certainly heightened the piety but also recast the isolated individual in a pedagogic register.[74] This is the figure that from the mid-nineteenth century onwards is used, according to Michael White,

to depict a number of processes whereby limited resources are allocated among alternative uses. The composition of output, for example, is dependent upon the economic agent's preferences or desires . . . the early marginalist treated the analysis of production in terms of the agent's decision to allocate his time to work, which was in turn dependent upon the relation between the satisfaction (utility) gained from the output and the pain (disutility) or work . . . As a utility maximizer, the agent is able to make fine distinctions and hence decisions at the margin among the various possibilities . . . economics becomes subjectivized in that wants are conceptualized as preferences for utilities which are in turn equivalent to what the agent desires. Those desires have no conditions of existence other than that they are preferred by the agent.[75]

Or, in Watson's words, 'the distinguishing feature of agents who maximise at the margin in economic theory is that they have all of their history taken away from them'.[76] This is really the point that Marx was making when he first raised the Crusoe figure in his 1847 tirade against Proudhon's theorising of economic value, 'to illustrate . . . a situation in which the *social* element had been reduced to a minimum'.[77]

Marx, who almost certainly read Campe before Defoe—the original German edition of *Das Kapital* has Crusoe raising llamas, not goats—would have found an even juicier target in Frédéric Bastiat—one of 'the modern bagmen of free trade'—whose *Economic Sophisms* of 1845 was a critique of protectionism that would occasion his own polemic against Proudhon.[78] In a chapter entitled 'Something Else', Bastiat provides an early instance of marginalism through a dialogue between Crusoe and Friday (here fluent and on equal terms):

Some time later, after Robinson had met Friday, they pooled their resources and began to cooperate in common enterprises. In the morning, they hunted for six hours and brought back four baskets of game. In the evening, they worked in the garden for six hours and obtained four baskets of vegetables.

One day a longboat landed on the Isle of Despair. A handsome foreigner disembarked and was admitted to the table of our two recluses. He tasted and highly praised the products of the garden, and, before taking leave of the hosts, he addressed them in these words:

'Generous islanders, I dwell in a land where game is much more plentiful than it is here, but where horticulture is unknown. It will be easy for me to bring you four baskets of game every evening, if you will give me in exchange only two baskets of vegetables'.

At these words, Robinson and Friday withdrew to confer, and the debate they had is too interesting for me not to report it here in full.

Friday: Friend, what do you think of it?

Robinson: If we accept, we are ruined.

F.: Are you quite sure of that? Let us reckon up what it comes to.

R.: It has all been reckoned up, and there can be no doubt about the outcome. This competition will simply mean the end of our hunting industry.

F.: What difference does that make if we have the game?

R.: You are just theorizing! It will no longer be the product of our labor.

F.: No matter, since in order to get it we shall have to part with some vegetables!

R.: Then what shall we gain?

F.: The four baskets of game cost us six hours of labor. The foreigner gives them to us in exchange for two baskets of vegetables, which take us only three hours to produce. Therefore, this puts three hours at our disposal.

R.: You ought rather to say that they are subtracted from our productive activity. That is the exact amount of our loss. *Labor is wealth*, and if we lose one-fourth of our working time, we shall be one-fourth less wealthy.

F.: Friend, you are making an enormous mistake. We shall have the same amount of game, the same quantity of vegetables, and—into the bargain—three more hours at our disposal. That is what I call progress, or there is no such thing in this world.[79]

The exchange continues for two more pages, but it is clearly game, set and match to Friday, for whom mastery of economic 'logic' has provided a kind of double emancipation.

Bastiat's rather unusual exchange has some perverse veracity, as Fritz Sollner points out:

Robinson Crusoe never performs the kind of utility maximising calculations he is supposed to . . . he does not rationally allocate his time between work and leisure . . . contrary to the premises of neo-classical economics, leisure *per se* has no (or hardly any) value for him . . . For him . . . the marginal utility of labor is always positive and constant, and the marginal utility of leisure is always zero (or, if it is positive, constantly below that marginal utility of labor).

But if in this instance Bastiat is closer to Defoe's Crusoe, he still forms part of a neoclassical lineage in which

There are universally valid economic laws . . . for economics to become a 'real' science, on a par with the natural sciences, especially physics, it had to be based on laws and principles that must not in any way be dependent on historical circumstances or social conditions.[80]

This is the point that Marx insists upon in the first paragraph of his *Grundrisse* a decade after the palisade against Proudhon:

Individuals producing in society—hence socially determined individual production—is, of course, the point of departure. The individual and isolated hunter and fisherman, with whom Smith and Ricardo begin, belongs among the unimaginative conceits of the eighteenth-century Robinsonades, which in no way express merely a reaction against over-sophistication and a return to a misunderstood natural life, as cultural historians imagine . . . Smith and Ricardo still stand with both feet on the shoulders of the eighteenth-century prophets, in whose imaginations this eighteenth-century individual—the product on one side of the dissolution of feudal forms of society, on the other side of the new forces of production developed since the sixteenth century—appears as an ideal, whose existence they project into the past. Not as a historic result but as history's point of departure. As the Natural Individual appropriate to their notion of human nature, not arising historically, but posited by nature.

Marx evidently feels annoyed that he has to labour such an issue:

There is no point in dwelling on this any longer. The point could go entirely unmentioned if this twaddle, which had sense and reason for the eighteenth-century characters, had not been earnestly pulled back into the centre of the most modern economics by Bastiat, Carey, Proudhon etc.[81]

Yet, as we have seen, a decade later still, in the first volume of *Capital* Marx returns to Defoe—once citing his 1710 essay on public credit but far more substantially by moving through the *Robinsonaden* to Robinson Crusoe himself. Why? Because 'political economists are fond of Robinson Crusoe stories'.

Whether one function occupies a greater space in his total activity than another depends on the magnitude of the difficulties to be overcome in attaining the useful effect aimed at. Our friend Robinson Crusoe learns this by experience, and having saved a watch, ledger, ink and pen from the shipwreck, he soon begins, like a good Englishman, to keep a set of books. His stock-book contains a catalogue of the useful objects he possesses, of the various operations necessary for their production, and finally of the labour time that specific quantities of these products have on average cost him. All the relations between Robinson and these objects that form his self-created wealth are here so simple and transparent that even Mr Sedley Taylor could understand them. And yet those relations contain all the essential determinants of value.

And just as Marx starts to slip towards the demonstrative errors of the political economists, he pulls himself back to the main issue:

Let us now transport ourselves from Robinson's island, bathed in light, to medieval Europe, shrouded in darkness. Here, instead of the independent man, we find everyone dependent—serfs and lords, vassals and suzerains, laymen and clerics.[82]

In these later works S.S. Prawer discerns a tension between Marx's rebuttal of the use of the *Robinsonaden* to naturalise historical processes, on the one hand, and his respect, on the other, for the prophetic powers of great artists.

The older he grew, the more he came to agree with Hegel and the German idealists that truth lay below the level of immediate empirical perception. It had to be dug free by well-informed men with a gift for theorizing and philosophic reflection, or seized by the intuition of great artists . . . In his economic studies Marx follows Mandeville as well as Hegel in seeing *evil* as one of the great mothers of the arts.[83]

*

Whether in his earlier excoriation of the pretensions of science or in his later turn towards Romanticism, Karl Marx could not impede the neoclassical juggernaut building from the 1870s. First Jevons—'even Crusoe must have looked upon each of his possessions with varying esteem and desire for more'—through Marshall and Edgeworth, who depicted the Crusoe-Friday relationship as 'Pure Contract' in *Mathematical Psychics*, to Frank Knight, founder of the Chicago School, for whom

> The concept of a Crusoe economy seems to me to be almost indispensable . . . I do not see how we can talk sense about economics without considering the economic behaviour of an isolated individual.

For Knight and the formidable trail of neoclassical 'scientists' that followed him, the objective was precisely to identify a truly rational actor:

> Only in that way can we expect to get rid by abstraction of all personal relationships, mutual persuasion, personal antipathies, and consciously competitive or cooperative relationships which keep the behavior of an individual in society from being, in any closely literal sense, economically rational. Crusoe would be in

this position: he would actually use given means to achieve given ends, his purely individualistic wants.[84]

If such a man is one who has 'internalized, reified and deified the economic aspects of life', as in Marx's vision, then Daniel Defoe's invention did not himself evidently live up to scratch, but he provides a very good template for those who would continue to reinvent him three hundred years later.

Here Come the French (Intellectuals)

Please take a deep breath.

> Realism can only be, not the copy of things, but the knowledge of language; the most realistic work will not be the one which 'paints' reality, but which, using the world as a content (a content which is, incidentally, a stranger to its [the work's] content, that is to say, to its being), makes the deepest possible explanation of the unreal reality of the language.

This declaration from Roland Barthes's *Le Degré zero de l'ecriture* (1953) has, for Ian Watt, who translated it, an 'engaging finality'. Watt's appraisal of the analytic techniques of the 'structuralism' at the heart of the emergent French intellectual elite was not so distinct from Marx's view of the 'naturalism' of the political economists.

> It is concerned with timeless verities at a much deeper level than the particularities or individual literary works, and rejects as an

exploded—or at any rate rather dull—relic of the past the notion that the referential functions of language, and therefore the representational status of literature, any longer merit the attentions of a sophisticated mind . . . The essence of the system is to promote brilliantly idiosyncratic verbalization without any fixed or controlling relation to anything outside the Cartesian ego as it thinks: it is all *cogito* and no *cogitamos*. The only real external constraints are those which they share with the Parisian high fashion industry.[85]

If this deliberately arch judgement possesses a persuasive element and does not, as we will see, lose its acuity, the fact of the matter is that throughout the 1950s and 1960s the interests and procedures of Watt and Barthes converged appreciably. The latter engaged with texts directly, and from well outside the confines of books, and he embraced the notion of 'myth', albeit more as 'a type of speech' than as a socio-cultural inheritance. Moreover, Barthes was one of the most prominent members of the post-war French intelligentsia to view the appraisal of *Robinson Crusoe* as an important task. Whether undertaken directly or indirectly, this group also included Pierre Macherey, Gilles Deleuze and Jacques Derrida, who arguably read the book closest of all.

The first pass that Barthes made through this territory was indirect—with an appraisal of the *Nautilus*, the submarine craft of Captain Nemo invented by Jules Verne. Focusing on Verne's 'almost perfect novel', *L'Ile Mysterieuse* (1874–5), Barthes's brief essay of 1957 builds through a number of themes familiar to us from the analysis of *Crusoe*, around which Verne undertook a science fiction *pirouette*:

> Verne had an obsession for plenitude: he never stopped putting a last touch to the world and furnishing it with an egg-like fullness. His tendency is exactly that of an eighteenth-century encyclopae-dist or of a Dutch painter: the world is finite, the world is full of numerable and contiguous objects . . . Verne belongs to the progressive lineage of the bourgeoisie: his work proclaims that nothing can escape man, that the world, even its most distant part, is like an object in his hand, and that, all told, property is but a dialectical moment in the general enslavement of nature.

But he does not neglect the inner aspects that link Verne with Defoe:

> The *Nautilus* . . . is the most desirable of all caves: the enjoyment of being enclosed reaches its paroxysm when, from the bosom of this unbroken inwardness, it is possible to watch, through a large window-pane, the outside vagueness of the waters, and thus define, in a single act, the inside by means of its opposite . . . The object that is the true opposite of Verne's *Nautilus* is Rimbaud's *Drunken Boat*, the boat which says 'I' and, freed from its concavity, can make man proceed from a psycho-analysis of the cave to a genuine poetics of exploration.[86]

That's how the essay ends, which was far too allusive for Pierre Macherey, who in 1963 criticised Barthes's 'short cut', and sought to provide a 'thematic ancestry' of *L'Ile Mysterieuse* through a direct appreciation of *Robinson Crusoe*. Macherey does not dispute the important differences between the books— 'In some sense, *Robinson Crusoe* is the novel of passing time. Verne's characters . . . are always in a hurry'—but he insists upon the ancestral role of *Crusoe*:

> In 1719, that is to say, before his time, Defoe, that brilliant journalist, initiates—in all senses of the word, dynamic, ludic, publicising—the theme of the man on an island . . . He made the island the indispensable setting, the scene for an ideological motif which was only beginning to emerge . . . Crusoe's island is thus a genuine *anticipation*, an early form of what is not yet an actuality . . . Defoe is possibly the only author by proxy (*auteur d'anticipation*), in so far as he supplied his successors with images.[87]

Macherey has no need to pick up on the evolving debate among Anglo-Saxon scholars as to the dominant theme of the book. For him it is evident both that the 'Providence' is an obsessive presence and that 'The motor of genesis is *work*. *Robinson Crusoe* is primarily a novel about work, the first of its kind'. For Macherey,

> With his miraculously *innocent* gaze, which surveys the origins of society, art, industry, thought and manners, the man on the island holds a place alongside the child, the savage, the blind man, the statue . . . in the arsenal of 'metaphysical instruments', conceptual images.

These are the words of a man who, two years later, would be co-author (alongside Althusser, Balibar, and Ranciere) of *Reading Capital*, and it is not hard to see here a parsing of Marx: 'Crusoe teaches us that there is no state of nature; that the notion belongs with those other myths which have been successively denounced (providence, God, good, and evil)'.[88]

Roland Barthes returned to *Crusoe* in far greater detail in his 1977 lecture and seminar course at the College de France, *How to Live Together: Novelistic Simulations of Some Everyday Spaces*. A number of lines of inquiry are evident from the painstaking reconstruction of these sessions. At the core of Barthes's concerns is a term of his own invention—'idiorrhythmy', derived from *idios* (particular) and *Rhuthmos* (rhythm)—in an 'attempt to reconcile collective life with individual life, the independence of the subject with the sociability of the group'.[89] For the novels/fantasies Barthes takes to assist in the search for this 'life art', he chooses *Crusoe* and Gide's *The Confined Woman of Poitiers*, both of which are interpreted at a kind of mezzo level that assumes the audience's familiarity with the texts.

However, Barthes's analytical tool-kit extends further still, to include an alphabetical list of Greek terms (from *Akedia*, carelessness/indifference, to *xenos*, foreign/strange) as he weaves the more composite categories of *monosis* (solitary life), *anachoresis* (life at a distance/in retreat), and [a complete invention of his own] *koinobiosis* (shared/common life). Barthes distinguishes himself from 'the normal reader' by finding all events that impinge on Crusoe's solitude 'irritating', so there is only modest discussion of Friday and the final episodes on the island. What is more important for a student of semiology are the parameters of language:

Substitute for language: the parrot. Robinson Crusoe captures one, so that they can 'speak'. After many years of training—the parrot calls Robinson Crusoe very familiarly by name. = To solicit a familiar *You*? To create someone who says *You* to you? It's possible to fetishize an object by turning it into a person, a God, a term of interpellation: the parrot in *A Simple Heart*. But it's not possible to solicit a familiar *You* from an object. Whence the irreplaceable nature of Robinson Crusoe's parrot: through the fact of hearing his own name, Robinson doesn't lose sight of the fact that he's a human being.[90]

It was around that issue—the parameters between animality and sovereignty—that Jacques Derrida structured his seminar of 2002–3 at the Ecole des hautes etudes en sciences sociales in Paris. As with Barthes, Derrida chooses *Crusoe* as one of his explicatory texts, but the other is of a very different type—Heidegger's *The Fundamental Concepts of Metaphysics* of 1929–30. Yet if the texts are about as different in expressive style as it is possible to imagine, Derrida overlapped with Barthes in his concerns over solitude, insularity, violence, boredom, and death. Barthes had raised the issue of animals, but not centrally; for Derrida they are the heart of his analytical story.

The Beast and the Sovereign does, understandably, bear some impression of Barthes's ideas of a quarter of a century earlier. The issue of the parrot, Poll, returns—'first victim of the humanist arrogance that thought it could give itself the right to speech, and therefore the right to the world itself'.[91] For Derrida inhumanity is exclusively human. The book is exceptionally

"Robinson Crusoe and His Pets" lithograph by Currier & Ives, 1874.

complex, and one greatly appreciates the assistance of those who have deconstructed this arch deconstructionist and put him together again in non-parenthetical, less serpentine form. Still, once one surrenders to Derrida's flow of reflective consciousness, there are things seen and unseen (Macherey would say *non-dit*) to be appreciated. Let's take the key moment of the footprint in the sand.

> *Finally*, having put his Bible down and comforted himself through prayer, he asks where he is, in what place, what his path would have been. He then wonders even more anxiously if this bare footprint is not that of his own foot. His own foot on a path he has already taken. Just as Poll the parrot returns to him only the echo of his voice, so the bare footprint is the more *unheimlich*, uncanny, for being quite possibly his own, on a path already trodden, that he has always described without knowing it . . . He does not really know . . . Is it me? Is it my track? Is it my path? Is it the spectre of my print, the print of my spectre? Am I coming back? Am I or am I not returning? Am I a revenant of myself?[92]

There is, moreover, one telling passage towards the end where Derrida recounts a flu-induced reverie in which all the political leaders involved in the 2003 Gulf War are arraigned before an international tribunal, and he has to argue for their right to words; not just *logos semantikos* (simple speech) but also *logos apophantikos* (propositional, predictive, prayer-like words). In his dream Derrida argues that they all—even George W. Bush—should be granted both.

When I awoke, I wondered (but I still had the flu) what would happen if they locked all these Polls up, for example in isolation in that bit of the Island of Cuba called Guantánamo, to teach them how to speak, to have them follow an intensive course of education in *Robinson Crusoe*, a seminar of Heidegger's and Aristotle's *Peri hermeneias*. As soon as my fever went down, I had to recognize that that would change nothing in the current war, of course. And that there is no doubt no possible war, among other things, without *logos apophantikos*.

Derrida then surveys the ideas of Kant and Heidegger on such matters. But we can cut straight to the chase:

At bottom, all these people, from Defoe to Lacan via Heidegger, belong to the same world in which the animal is cut from man by a multiple defect of power (speech, dying, signifier, truth and lie, etc.). What Robinson thinks of his parrot Poll is pretty much what Descartes, Kant, Heidegger, Lacan, and so many others, think of all animals incapable of a true responsible and responding speech, of a *logos semantikos* and a *logos apophantikos*. [93]

If this is the effective conclusion of Derrida's magisterial survey, he opens it by looking equally askance at Lacan through the application of his ideas to the Robinsonade tradition by Gilles Deleuze, who in 1969 had concluded, 'We must imagine Robinson to be perverse; the only Robinsonade is perversion itself', on the grounds that 'the world of the pervert is a world without Other, and thereby a world without possibility'.[94] The capitalisation of

Other here is not simply at the service of Lacanian psychoanalysis but also in promotion of what we might call an 'anti-Crusoe'—Michel Tournier's *Vendredi ou les limbes du Pacifique* (*Friday or the Other Island*), the 1967 French edition of which contained Deleuze's essay as an afterward.

Deleuze, as we have seen, had a low opinion of Defoe's story, even as he recognised its power. Tournier's text, though, is a most effective subversion of the original:

> Tournier's Robinson is opposed to Defoe's in virtue of three strictly related characteristics: he is related to ends and goals rather than origins; he is sexual; and these ends represent a fantastic deviation from our world, under the influence of a transformed sexuality, rather than an economic reproduction of our world, under the impact of continuous effort.[95]

Deleuze fortifies this distinction with a direct quote from Tournier, who in the final pages of *Vendredi/Friday* 'quotes' from a journal written by his Robinson:

> My love-affair with Speranza [the island] was still largely human in its nature; I fecundated her soil as if I were lying with a wife. It was Friday who brought about the deeper change. The harsh stab of desire that pierces the loins of a lover has been transformed for me into soft jubilation which exalts and pervades me from head to foot, so long as the sun-god bathes me in his rays. There is no longer that loss of substance that leaves the animal, *post coitum,*

sad. My sky-love floods me with a vital energy which endows me with strength for a day and a night. If this is to be translated into human language, I must consider myself feminine and the bride of the sky. But that kind of anthropomorphism is meaningless. The truth is that at the height to which Friday and I have soared difference of sex has been left behind. Friday may be identified with Venus, just as I may be said, in human terms, to open my body to the embrace of the sun.[96]

Such celestial intercourse might have been influenced by Fourier, whose *New Amorous World* was posthumously published in 1967 and who was content not only with a third sex but also inter-planetary fornication. It might even have been intelligible to Alexander Selkirk, readily imagined ejaculating hither and thither in capricornian copulation as a sovereign with no human Others. If it is on the very frontier of an imagination we might attribute to Daniel Defoe—*Conjugal Lewdness: or, Matrimonial Whoredom* is built upon *non-dits* but *Moll Flanders* and *Roxana* have some quite hard-core moments—it did not exhaust Michel Tournier's engagement with the Robinsonade since four years later he published *Vendredi: ou la vie sauvage/Friday and Robinson: Life on Speranza Island* as a version for children. 'Children', he said, 'are not afraid of the big questions', but here their sensuality is addressed 'in real time', through food, bodily functions, and the softness of bedclothes.[97]

Tournier's two-hander is a rare example of subverting both Defoe and Campe. It is in the nature of the first revolt—based on an implicitly Freudian understanding of sexual development but fiercely counterposed to any heterosexual norm of behaviour—that the second proved to be a necessary undertaking.

The Modern Literary Legacy

Tournier's *Friday* opens as a seemingly conventional permutation of the *Crusoe* canon with readily intelligible adjustments to the surface narrative. Here Robinson is transported in time to 30 September 1759, a century later than Defoe's castaway, allowing some extra historical space in which to reflect upon the Enlightenment tradition. Benjamin Franklin's writings are cited, whereas in historical time it was Franklin who discussed Defoe's work. Slightly lower beneath the surface, Tournier's Robinson has been three years on the island when Rousseau published *Émile*, the whole civilisational thrust of which is one of Tournier's central targets.

There are secondary shifts—we are back in the Pacific, on Selkirk's island, and the visiting indigenous people are Araucanians from the mainland who sacrifice but do not eat their victims; eating is very much a property of Robinson's behaviour, which is alleviated by the possession of fire from the start, of a dog, Tenn, but no Poll. However, a few early notes signal a less prosaic set of motifs up ahead. Before his ship (the *Virginia*) is wrecked, Robinson has the tarot explained to him by the captain, who turns up the Capricorn, 'the door which is the soul's way out—that is to say, death'. But when the ship goes down it is Robinson who alone survives, the captain's last words being, 'Beware of purity. It is corrosive of the soul'. The goat theme remains until the final pages. Robinson clubs to death the first one he meets. In his republican version of Defoe's monarchist administrative phase, Tournier has Robinson carefully number off the nanny-goats for assigned mating with the billies, and he later muses wistfully about writing words on their coats.

However, before Robinson enters that stage of the existential cycle where he is drafting constitutions, instituting penal codes, and building a chapel, one side of which is reserved for non-existent women, he surrenders to nature and enters the mire:

> The thought of sunburn no longer trouble, since his back, flanks and thighs were now protected by a thick coating of dried mud . . . He lived on unmentionable foods, gnawing them with his face to the ground. He relieved himself where he lay, and rarely failed to roll in the damp warmth of his own excrement.[98]

It is in escaping this state that Robinson declares his island is to be Esperanza, hope, rather than Despair. But he has yet to discover through his immersion in the cave, covered in goat's milk, that he is also inside his mother. And when, resting warmly within, his semen runs free, he only just manages to stop it sealing the spell of life and death into which he has entered. Tournier has an assured knowledge of the Bible and quotes it much more fully than Defoe, but we are now also in the land of polymorphous perversity that Deleuze appreciated. The Old Testament metaphors mound up, so that, safely on the surface, Robinson can now reflectively incubate two persons—the man who needs a woman and the man who must fecundate the plants and soil.

Yet this is not a steady state. In his journal Robinson records that as the parameters of his desire are transformed, so have words:

> To say that my sexual desire is no longer directed towards the perpetuation of the species is not enough. It no longer knows what its purpose is! For a long time memory was sufficiently active in me to feed my imagination with objects of desire, non-existent though they were. But that is now over. Memory has been sucked dry. The creatures of my imagination are lifeless shadows. I may speak the words, woman, breasts, thighs, thighs parted at my desire, but they mean nothing. Words have lost their image; they are sounds, no more.[99]

Friday's arrival alters but does not halt this process, and the final stages of Tournier's tale open in marked contradistinction to Defoe's narrative change of gears. When Friday escapes from the sacrifice being prepared for him, Robinson decides to shoot him, not his pursuers, as this would be more judicious in terms of his own survival. Only the fact that the dog knocks him off balance means that it is one of the pursuing Araucanians who is killed, Friday, the mixed race negro-Araucanian, surviving. And he is a laughing boy, submissive but wilfully carefree in nature; he can be made obedient through violence but he internalises no more than that strictly necessary for cohabitation. When Friday kills the great goat Andaor, with skill and innate patience he converts its hide into a kite and its skull into a wind-strummed Aeolian harp. Encouraged by his reading of the Bible and his growing admiration of Friday's communion with nature, Robinson moves towards companionship.

Friday was Tournier's first novel, but it was published when he was forty-three and had accumulated plenty of experience as a script-writer following his thwarted graduate studies in philosophy. The moral tales here have various valencies. The denouement really begins when Friday, smoking tobacco furtively inside—he never did so outside—sets off a huge explosion of Robinson's gunpowder, kills the dog, and begins his 'master's' further transformation in the cutting of his hair and the assumption of a meekness almost beyond admiration. Then the ship arrives.

Friday sold three million copies in France and was Tournier's 'lucky book', allowing him to spend the rest of a long life (1924–2016) as an independent author. Perhaps of all the twentieth-century 'renovations' of *Robinson Crusoe*, it was the most radical rewriting, but it was also one of the most artful, and the final pages enclose further twists of the plot that are best left to the original. These are incorporated into *Friday and Robinson*, which is purged of the sex and so, as might be expected, a corresponding deviation from the dynamics of Defoe's original.

In *Friday*, Tournier had effectively settled accounts with the qualities of *Crusoe* listed by James Joyce fifty years earlier:

. . . the whole Anglo-Saxon spirit; the manly independence; the unconscious cruelty; the persistence; the slow yet efficient intelligence; the sexual apathy; the practical, well-balanced religiousness; the calculating taciturnity.[100]

Small wonder, perhaps, that Joyce's own characters took on quite different registers. On the other hand, that other great writer of early twentieth-century English prose, Virginia Woolf, was able to see in the original some of the tactile, telluric features in Defoe that Tournier sought to turn against him:

> Defoe, by reiterating that nothing but a plain earthenware pot stands in the foreground, persuades us to see remote islands and the solitudes of the human soul. By believing fixidly in the solidity of the pot and its earthiness, he has subdued every element to his design; he has roped the whole universe into harmony.[101]

Tournier's book was also bracketed by the publication of two great poems in English that 'reconvened' Crusoe sympathetically in different spaces. Derek Walcott's 'Crusoe's Island' (1965) assumes a firm Caribbean setting, but does not evacuate the religiosity from the scene:[102]

> Upon this rock the bearded hermit built
> His Eden:
> Goats, corn crop, fort, parasol, garden,
> Bible for Sabbath, all the joys
> But one
> Which sent him howling for a human voice.
> Exiled by a flaming sun
> The rotting nut, bowled in the surf,
> Became his own brain rotting from the guilt
> Of heaven without his kind,

CRUSOE

Crazed by such paradisal calm
The spinal shadow of a palm
Built keel and gunwale in his mind . . .

Elizabeth Bishop surely was familiar with these lines when, over a decade later, she composed 'Crusoe in England', providing a clean, direct account of essentials:[103]

I often gave way to self-pity.
"Do I deserve this? I suppose I must.
I wouldn't be here otherwise. Was there
a moment when I actually chose this?
I don't remember, but there could have been."
What's wrong with self-pity, anyway?
With my legs dangling down familiarly
over a crater's edge, I told myself
"Pity should begin at home." So the more
pity I felt, the more I felt at home . . .

These are exceptional, condensed literary moments in a lineage that is as broad as it is deep if we include recognisable permutations such as those written by William Golding (both *Pincher Martin* and *Lord of the Flies*), Muriel Spark (*Robinson*), and J.G. Ballard (*Concrete Island*) or the appreciable filmic output from Burbank's sundry castaways to *Lost in Space*, let alone when we inquire how Wells's *The Island of Dr. Moreau*, itself a substantial re-imagining, was further fantasised in *The Invention of Morel* by Bioy Casares, and the impact that exercised on Borges.[104] Two further texts, though, do deserve some consideration for the manner in which they addressed, first, the compositional legacy of *Crusoe* and, secondly, its symbolic role within the existential rhythms of twentieth-century England.

*

Foe, published by the South African author J.M. Coetzee in 1986, is a tight, taut novel concerned with composition—not just that of some alternative *Robinson Crusoe* but also of Defoe's later novel *Roxana* (1724), with motifs of each inverted and interlaced in a barely sub-cutaneous essay on language and power. The book is arguably mistitled; Foe does not speak at all for nearly two-thirds of the book. The first-person narrator is one Susan Barton, who spends much time addressing herself to Foe in letters to get him to craft a fluent written version of her stay on the island with Cruso— spelled as real-life Timothy was—and Friday, who, in the central figure of the book, cannot speak as his tongue has been cut out. Friday is described on the first page as a Negro.

This is a story that does not need to be spoiled for those yet to read it, but it won't be much of a nuisance to know that Cruso, who keeps no journal and exhibits a 'stubbornness of old age' on the island, dies at sea having been 'rescued'. There is no seed or cultivation, except of unproductive stone terraces. The island is swept sharply by the wind.

Coetzee's serial revelation of paths not taken in the text is imbricated with a lightly traced biography of Foe/Defoe in which Susan and Friday squat in his Stoke Newington home, abandoned by the owner in flight from his creditors. So, when we are sitting comfortably we can savour the sense of Coetzee writing about Susan writing to Foe about his own writing:

> Your papers are kept in a chest beside the table. The story of Cruso's island will go there page by page as you write it, to lie with a heap of other papers: a census of the beggars of London, bills of mortality from the time of the great plague, accounts of travel in the border country, reports of strange and surprising apparitions, records of the wool trade, a memorial of the life and opinions of Dickory Cronke (who is he?); also books of voyages to the New World, memoirs of captivity among the Moors, chronicles of the wars in the Low Countries, confessions of notorious lawbreakers, and a multitude of castaway narratives, most of them, riddled with lies.[105]

Coetzee continued to have his own fun with creative lies when, in the 2003 acceptance speech of the Nobel prize for literature—'He and His Man'—he took his distinguished audience down different paths, in character and recognisable as those of Crusoe and Friday. Now, though, Friday has written about decoy ducks in the English fenlands, and Crusoe has retreated to solitude in the bedroom of a Bristol inn. The matter of composition lingers:

> When, years ago, he resolved to set down on paper the story of his island, he found that the words would not come, the pen would not flow, his very fingers were stiff and reluctant. But day by day,

step by step, he mastered the writing business, until by the time of his adventures with Friday in the frozen north the pages were rolling off easily, even thoughtlessly.[106]

For those yearning for some third-person exteriority Coetzee provides a little relief in an essay on *Roxana* in which he takes issue with the judgement on Defoe made by Hippolyte Taine in 1863:

> It is in [avoiding the appearance of fiction] that his talent lies. In this way his imperfections serve his interest. His oversights, his repetitions, his prolixity contribute to the illusion; we cannot claim that such and such a detail, so petty, so dull, could be invented—an inventor would have left it out, it is too tedious to have been put in on purpose. Art makes choices, embellishes, engages our interest; art could not possibly have piled up this load of dull, vulgar particulars; therefore it must be the truth.

Coetzee allows a quite full quotation—there is another one too—in a short essay because it represents the mainstream critical view of Defoe's artifice:

> Taine's verdict on Defoe is a harsh one, yet in essence it persists to the present day. As a writer Defoe did not know what he was doing, therefore he could have had no idea of the importance of what he was doing. Instead, following intuitions that, in retrospect, we concede may have flowed from a certain inborn genius, he gave us, under a series of disguises, a representation of the mind of his age, or rather, the mind of an important social

actor: the inquisitive, acquisitive man or woman of the ascendant Protestant middle class.

Here Coetzee sounds quite like Watt, but as a writer of fictions himself, he ends with a celebration of the conundrums involved in being the founder of the guild:

> Defoe had no models for the kind of extended fiction he was writing: he was not only making up the story as he went along, he was making up the form too. Although it cannot be proved, there is every reason to believe he wrote at speed and with little revision. It would be wrong to say that the last sixty or seventy pages of *Roxana* were written in a state of possession—Defoe was too clear-minded, too intelligent, too professional for that. But he was certainly writing beyond his powers, beyond what either he or his contemporaries thought him capable of.[107]

*

There is a Poll right at the centre of Jane Gardam's *Crusoe's Daughter* (1985). She is Polly Flint, born in the last years of the nineteenth century, soon orphaned, and sequestered with two errant maiden aunts (Frances and Mary Younghusband) in the northeast of England, where she lives out most of her long life, occasionally directly affected by the crises and conflicts of the twentieth century—nearby Hartlepool is bombed; a poet who courts her dies early in the trenches; the engaging Zeit family makes the tragic miscalculation of returning to Germany after the Great War. All the while,

Polly is protected by *Robinson Crusoe*. She writes to Frances of a rare visit to Yorkshire and an exchange with the effete Lady Celia over the merits of Tennyson (the sound of Tournier's dog resonates in this quietly ludic text):

> 'Well, I don't think he's quite as good as Daniel Defoe.'
> 'Daniel *Defoe*?' she said, as if other Daniels might have got by—
> the one in the lions den, or the one George Eliot wrote about. Or
> Daniel the Upright and Discerning Judge.
> 'Daniel *Defoe*? You mean *Robinson Crusoe*? *Moll Flanders*?'
> 'Yes.'
> 'But my child—no trace, no *trace* of poetry. No trace of poetic
> truth.'
> But then, Aunt Frances, I grew terribly angry and said in a fury,
> '*Robinson Crusoe* is full of poetic truth. And it is an attempt at a
> universal truth very differently expressed.'
> 'No form,' she cried, 'no form.'
> I said, 'It is wonderfully written. It is true to his chosen form.
> Because of this verisimilitude it reads like reality. I have read
> it twenty-three times. In a novel form is not always apparent
> at a first or second reading. Form is determined by hard secret
> work—in a notebook and in the subconscious and in the head.'[108]

Here Polly is telling us that we the readers must match Defoe the writer and Crusoe the castaway for effort. Goodbye Michel Tournier; try harder Susan Barton.

Right on the cusp of war Paul Treece, the doomed suitor, takes a different tack on Crusoe:

> '. . . he was afraid of everything. Sleeping up trees, building fortresses with secret back-doors—and after years—years—when he'd never been troubled by any living creature, he gets the shakes over a dying goat. After he spotted the foot-print he had the shakes for two whole years. And he only started praying out of fright. He prays non-stop for twenty-eight years—*out of fright*. He never sits still. He's a bundle of nerves. He lives in fear, refined and pure. He's magnificent when the shooting starts, I agree. Smell of cordite, whites of eyes and so forth. But for a quarter of century, waiting for the fun to start, he's a dithering, boring coward.'
>
> 'Perhaps he did have some imagination then.'[109]

This is the last conversation between Polly and Paul before he goes off to die. Sometimes the spirit of Austen hovers over the grey picaresque process of Polly's existence up to 1939, when, in a *Crusoe*-like gear change from a cycle of vitally banal personal stories on the edge of the North Sea, the Zeit children suddenly need collecting from the *Kindertransport* ship in London—salvation from the barbarians. Polly is barely forty; half her life is yet to come. But Gardam's novel is all but done. There is a suitably romantic twist in a 10-page coda, 'The End', when we are fast-forwarded to 1986. Rebecca Zeit/Beccy Boagley fails to get a journalist, Charlotte Box, into Polly's flat because she is now too deaf to hear the intercom and too distracted to find the key. Outside Beccy gives Charlotte a condensed account of Polly's life after the war, and then they go off to look for the key from the nuns in whose care Polly now lives.

We don't need to worry that Polly cannot tell Charlotte herself because Gardam has helped her tell the story to us. So, she now sits down, very tired and rather confused:

POLLY FLINT   I was looking—what was I looking for? I don't know—losing things, forgetting things. The key. And I knew she was coming, the journalist. Dear Charlotte Box. For my memoirs.

CRUSOE   My creator was a great believer in memoirs.

POLLY FLINT   So impossible, so false. Talking about memories.

CRUSOE   Oh, I don't know. My creator had quite a facility. Stood him in very good stead. Memoirs.

POLLY FLINT   Nonsense—he made it all up. Fiction isn't memory.

CRUSOE   But memory is fiction. I tell you my creator had no compunction—well, here I am, for a start.

POLLY FLINT   Making things up from nothing is another matter. An easier matter.

CRUSOE   He didn't quite do that. I am not sure that it was easy, exactly. I believe I quite tired him. Even God had to rest on the Seventh Day.

POLLY FLINT	Your creator must have been ready for a rest by the end of Book Three. I'll concede that.
CRUSOE	He said something of the sort. He said that I tended to take charge.
POLLY FLINT	You are apt to do that.
CRUSOE	Can't think why. I'm very ordinary.
POLLY FLINT	Yes—Dickens thought so.
CRUSOE	Never met him.
POLLY FLINT	I never thought so, though. You've lasted me out, Crusoe . . .[110]

*

DANIEL DEFOE

Daniel Defoe was born in the city of London probably in the autumn of 1660, possibly on 30 September. He was definitely born as Daniel Foe, the third child and only son of James (1630–1706) and Alice Foe. Daniel changed his name to DeFoe in 1695, but the currently uncapitalised 'f' was not used in his lifetime. His many enemies were inclined to use 'Foe' if only to scorn the pretensions of gentility implied by the frenchification. Sometimes in his letters he signed off as D. Foe. Alice Foe, whom Daniel mentions only once in his writings, died before 1671, with James remarrying one Elizabeth. They, like Daniel, are today buried in Bunhill Fields, the Dissenters' cemetery off City Road. It is worth noting at the outset that much of what Daniel did up until December 1706—including being an outlawed rebel, incurring two distinct bankruptcies (still treated as criminal acts), and serving two terms in prison for both debt and sedition—would have taken place under the eyes of his father, whose funeral he could not attend because he was in Edinburgh serving as a secret agent for the English government in promoting a united kingdom with Scotland.

We cannot be sure of Daniel's date of birth because, like his sisters (whose births were simply noted), he was not baptised in the family's parish church of St. Giles, Cripplegate, possibly because Alice was a Quaker and so opposed to the use of oaths, whereas James was a Presbyterian and simply opposed to the use of the cross at baptism. However, the matter became entirely irrelevant after the 1662 Act of Uniformity, which required all priests to subscribe to the Thirty-Nine Articles of the Church of England, be ordained by a bishop, use the Book of Common Prayer for all services and 'assent to all and every thing contained and prescribed' in it. This resulted in the expulsion of perhaps two thousand clerics—Defoe later claimed three thousand—many of them followed by the devout Dissenters in their congregations, perhaps seven per cent of an English population of around 5.5 million.[1] The Foe family followed their vicar, the Reverend Samuel Annesley, who had been appointed three years before by Richard Cromwell, out of the established church and in doing so lost any opportunity to hold any public office, including that of teacher, to attend university, or even to worship in public, for which stiff fines were imposed on Nonconformists. Daniel was then too young to register the political enormity of this religious conflict, and we are today perhaps too secularised to grasp fully its salience to both public and private life in the late seventeenth century, even if we recall that the Act, and the rest of the 'Clarendon Code' introduced early in the reign of Charles II, was imposed barely a dozen years after the Civil War, in which nearly two hundred thousand people died, and the execution of Charles I.

By the time Defoe was drafting *Robinson Crusoe*, divisions within English Protestantism had lost much of their sharpness, but even after the abortive effort of 1715 to install a Catholic (Jacobite) Pretender on the

British crown, the issue of monarchical succession was not completely settled, the Scottish-based pretensions of the Stuart family were incompletely extinguished, and militant anti-papism was still at the heart of mainstream culture. Much of Daniel Defoe's adult life, therefore, was conducted amidst conflicts that had not been assuaged by the 'Glorious Revolution' of 1688, the Bill of Rights of 1689, William III's defeat of James II at the Battle of the Boyne in 1690, or the succession of James's Protestant daughter Anne in 1702. Nobody seriously suggests that he could remember the Plague of 1665, his Uncle Henry's accounts being the most likely source of *A Journal of the Plague Year* (1722), but it is unlikely that, as a fourteen-year-old, he was unaffected by the death of John Milton, who had defended the execution of Charles I, and who is buried in St. Giles, where his bust stands alongside those of Defoe and Oliver Cromwell. And Daniel was married with a daughter at the death in 1688 of John Bunyan, the author of *Pilgrim's Progress* who had served eleven years in Bedford Jail for his dissenting beliefs, and who Defoe may, as a schoolboy, have heard preach at Newington Green.

New controversies, of course, sprang up over the following decades, not least over British involvement in the European wars of 1689–97 and 1702–1713, occasioning a financial revolution and conflicts over foreign policy so sharp that they led to ministers being imprisoned in the Tower of London on charges of sedition as well as assassination attempts. Yet, aside from his often obscure and almost always failed business dealings, Daniel Defoe mostly got into trouble—serious trouble threatening judicial execution as well as vigilante violence—over religious matters and their political implications. So, although the doctrinal landscape of over three hundred years ago is complex as well as alien, we do have to recognise that it was just as important to those living at the time as, say, Brexit or Trump are today. Certainly, there were moments when it instilled in Daniel Defoe the sheer fear and recurrent anxiety that he inserted into the mind and heart of Robinson Crusoe.

Surviving Stuart Supremacism

Michael Foot was absolutely right to describe Daniel Defoe as a tradesman, not a gentleman. And Tom Paulin had a point when he identified Defoe with a bourgeois revolution because this man who never entirely stopped playing the market and wholesaling, even in his last months, was a life-long Londoner as well as an ardent proponent of the 'Glorious Revolution'. Of course, in the 1720s Stoke Newington was still separated from the city by fields, as were Hackney and Kingsland, where he had lived previously. However, Defoe's life until he was nearly forty was spent in and around Cornhill, close to his parents' home. His appetite for the market must have been awakened at an early age by the fact that James Foe was a successful tallow chandler—a wholesale merchant of candles manufactured from animal fat—whose skilled industry led to appreciable prosperity and respectability, including leadership of the Butcher's Company. In time Foe would himself acquire the profile of 'gentleman' that so eluded his son, and he diversified his activities, not least because he had a talent for accounting—again something that Daniel conspicuously lacked throughout his life. However, it is fair to say that father and son shared a religious calling, and it is this that dominated Defoe's outlook and his public life well into adulthood.

As we have seen, less than two years after the Stuart Restoration in 1660, Nonconformists, who were disproportionately represented amongst London's merchant class, were targeted by the 'Penal Laws' overseen by the Earl of Clarendon. Amongst the earliest of these was the Corporation Act of December 1661, which prohibited anybody (any man) from being legally elected to any office relating to a town, city or corporation unless they had in the previous twelve months received the sacrament of 'the Lord's Supper' (Holy Communion) according to the rites of the Church of England. Additionally, nobody was eligible for any local office unless they had taken the Oath of Allegiance and Oath of Supremacy and sworn belief in Passive Obedience to the restored monarch. The impact of just this first measure was of such fierce restriction on the civil organisation of a minority group that, even if expressed in narrowly doctrinal terms, it is recognisable to those familiar with modern authoritarianism.

Within six months the Corporation Act was followed by that of Uniformity, which effectively expelled Presbyterians from the Church of England. As all Nonconformists were driven to develop a parallel sphere of religiosity, some simultaneously deployed 'the weapons of the weak' by playing the new system, taking Communion in the established Church in a practice known as 'Occasional Conformity'. The restored Episcopalian order and High Churchmen were stymied by this latter practice, against which some Dissenters, including Daniel Defoe, also argued on the grounds that it was an opportunistic suspension of principle. However, no measure to suppress Occasional Conformity was approved by Parliament until 1711, so some form of co-existence proved possible, albeit by dint of subterfuge. On the other hand, the regime moved quite early to suppress collective practice of dissenting Protestantism, the Conventicle Act of 1664 prohibiting all 'conventicles' (religious ceremonies of more than five people other than immediate family) outside the auspices of the Church of England. The following year the Five Mile Act forbade any ex-clergy from living within that distance of their previous parish. In sum, the first years of Charles II's reign imposed both repressive restrictions and a measure of geographical dislocation upon Nonconformists (not to mention Roman Catholics and Jews, who once again had a presence in London). The Defoe family stayed tight, but the climate of apprehension and fear that courses through passages of *Robinson Crusoe* surely suffused Daniel's early years. Indeed, he recalled that as a child, faced with the widespread fear of Catholic restoration and a suppression of the Bible, he had written up the Pentateuch (the first five books of the Old Testament) in order to commit them to memory. Annesley soon lost his goods for keeping a conventicle, but he continued as an itinerant preacher around Spitalfields and Shoreditch until the fall of James II brought him back into open Protestant culture, if not the Church of England.

Of course, even the devoutly Catholic James II, who succeeded his older brother in 1685, did not seek a reversal of the English Protestant Order—the great bulk of the population worshipped in England's ninety-five hundred Anglican parishes that underpinned the state—but it was not at all clear in the early 1660s that something of that order might not be essayed. Moreover, the five hundred thousand people who inhabited London were further traumatised by the Great Plague of 1665, when up to one hundred thousand were killed in under three months, and the Fire of London of September 1666, when many fewer died but ninety churches were destroyed. The Foe family was not listed amongst those burned out, but it would have left a deep impression on a six-year-old, even if Daniel did not witness as much as John Evelyn:

> The Conflagration was so universal, and the people so astonish'd, that from the beginning (I know not by what desponding or fate), they hardly stirr'd to quench it, so as there was nothing heard or seene but crying out and lamentation, and running about like distracted creatures, without at all attempting to save even their goods . . . God grant mine eyes may never behold the like, who now saw above ten thousand houses all in one flame, the noise and crakling and thunder of the impetuous flames, the shrieking of Women and children, the hurry of people, the fall of towers, houses and churches was like an hideous storme . . .[2]

The efforts to contain Nonconformism varied according to political circumstances, but at no time were they fiercer than during the 'Exclusion Crisis' of 1681–83, when Charles dismissed Parliament in the face of a largely Whig-driven campaign (and one assassination plot) to prevent James Stuart from succeeding to the throne after his brother because of his Catholicism. The widely-respected Dissenting divine Richard Baxter was jailed for breaking the Five-Mile Act in 1682 against the wishes of a number of Anglican bishops, and such was the repression that in February 1683 Narcissus Luttrell reported of London,

> The conventicles in and around this citty are prosecuted more violently than ever, so that even those that doe meet, doe it either early in the morning or late at night; notwithstanding which severall of them have been disturbed, and the principall hearers taken, and made to pay the penalties the law has inflicted.[3]

Perhaps eight thousand Dissenters were imprisoned, amongst them Thomas Delaune who, as Defoe noted several times in his later writing, died in Newgate Prison early in 1684, having witnessed the death of his wife and two children there because he was unable to pay the fine to secure the family's release. Some twenty years later, when Defoe was himself locked up in the same gaol, he understandably made sure that a down payment of twenty guineas and then twelve shillings a week ensured him quarters protected from rampant disease. Like Ian Watt, Daniel Defoe knew that it was hard to be prisoner, but at least he had the chance to buy some improvements.

Defoe did not by any means develop his religious and secular education exclusively within the context of adversity. Denied by the Penal Acts from attending Oxford and Cambridge, the only universities in England at the time, young Dissenters had the option of being educated abroad— Leiden was a favourite, not least because it offered training in medicine—or in their own academies. James Foe first sent Daniel to a school in Dorking, Surrey, and then, probably on the advice of Rev. Annesley, who had attended Oxford before him, to Charles Morton's academy at

Newington Green. Known as a mathematician at Oxford, Morton not only upheld the general academy practice of lecturing in English but also a curriculum much broader than at the 'ancient universities', including modern languages, politics, natural science, mathematics, and geography and history as well as religion and classics. Perhaps the best of the academies in England, Morton's accepted up to fifty students a year. Many, including Daniel at the start, attended to prepare for the Presbyterian ministry.

In a text, *The Compleat English Gentleman*, written in 1729 but not published until the late nineteenth century, Defoe gives us a pretty telling account of how his education by Morton fed into his later writing style:

> He had a class for eloquence, and his pupil's declaim'd weekly in the English tongue, made orations, and wrot epistles every week upon such subjects as he prescrib'd to them or upon such as they themselves chose to write upon. Sometimes they were ambassadors and agents abroad at foreign Courts, and wrote accounts of their negociations and recepcion in foreign Courts directed to the Secretary of State and sometimes to the Sovereign himself . . . Thus he taught his pupils to write a masculine and manly stile, to write the most polite English, and at the same time to kno' how to suit their manner as well to the subject . . . and all equally free and plain, without foolish flourishes and ridiculous flights of jingling bombast in stile, or dull meanesses of expression below the dignity of the subject or the character of the writer.[4]

This was not quite a training for *Crusoe* but it certainly set Defoe up well for writing his (secret) reports to Robert Harley from 1704. Morton did not live to see the published fruits of his teaching, being forced to migrate to Massachusetts in 1685, where he became vice-president of Harvard and died in April 1698, likely not seeing Defoe's *An Essay Upon Projects* issued in London a few months earlier.

Sometimes too much is made of the fact that the academies taught the work of John Locke when that was still prohibited at Oxford and Cambridge. This is because, under persecution and in exile, most of Locke's major writings were only published following the overthrow of the Stuart regime in 1688, when Daniel Defoe had long since finished his training. However, *An Essay Concerning Toleration*, composed in 1667 but never published in Locke's lifetime, expresses the tone and substance of the critique of absolutism under its sway:

> There are some that tell us that monarchy is *iure divino*. I will not now dispute this opinion, but only mind the asserters of it that if they mean by this (as certainly they must) that the sole, supreme, arbitrary power and disposal of all things is and ought to be by divine right in a single person, 'tis to be suspected they have forgot what country they are born in, under what laws they live, and certainly cannot but be obliged to declare Magna Carta to be downright heresy.[5]

Defoe would pick up on this theme in 1706 in his vast poetic polemic *Jure Divino*, but he mentioned Locke quite scarcely and not at all in his surviving

Newington Green. Photo by Sarah Ainslie.

letters. Moreover, we should be wary of any neat dichotomy between some secular rationalism in dissenting circles and a feudal mysticism prevailing in court and Church. The general limits to knowledge muddled many things up, not least when little or nothing was known of the interiors of several continents or even the coastlines of northwest Japan and northwest America. One simple consequence of this was the inability to explain the migration of birds, which Morton surmised spent the winter on the moon.[6]

There is no clear explanation for why the young Defoe did not proceed to the ministry, but neither is it really a huge mystery, either on a personal basis or in terms of the politico-religious climate of the 1670s and 1680s. Perhaps he lacked Timothy Cruso's talent for sermons, and already knew that the written word would be his forte? Moreover, he had the compelling examples of James Foe's success—trading in candles in one of the world's largest cities long before the advent of gas and electricity ran little risk of a collapse in demand, and supply was assured by London's carnivorous appetite. Not only had James diversified, but his brother Henry, a saddle-maker, had established strong trans-Atlantic ties with the growing colonies of North America that as much moved on horseback as they settled in cabins. Indeed, Daniel's subsequent life would prove to be more mobile and equestrian than might be imagined. He traded in horses when serving as an agent in Scotland, and again in the 1720s. His real tour of England in 1705 was necessarily conducted on horseback, as were his wider fictional travels in *A Tour Through the Whole Island of Great Britain* (1724). When arrested in 1713 he was permitted to ride from Stoke Newington to Newgate because he was suffering from a cold; and his apparent failure to pay for a horse to replace a lame animal in Coventry was picked up as a charge by his critics. When his businesses boomed, one of the first acquisitions was a coach, which was also the first item of conspicuous consumption to be sold off in the almost inevitable bust that would follow. In 1695 Gregory King estimated that there were 1.2 million horses in England, or roughly one for every four humans.[7]

As we already know, Daniel Defoe was difficult to follow, even in his own day. But it is evident that by the early 1680s he was succeeding as a wholesaler in woollen goods, as well as trading further afield in wines and brandy, principally with Spain and Portugal, and tobacco with North America. Defoe's travels abroad are almost completely unknown, and if it is certain that he never sailed in one of his ships to the American colonies, it is much less clear if he spent time in France, Spain, Portugal, or the Dutch republic, where he had commercial and religious ties. He might have travelled to Italy and had always shown a keen interest in French affairs. In 1705, riled by Tutchin's disparagement of his linguistic skills, Defoe challenged 'his rival to translate one Latin, one French, and one Italian author into English and then to retranslate each, "the *English* into *French*, the *French* into Italian, *and the Italian* into *Latin*"', and whoever did it quickest and best would owe the other £20. Tutchin did not take up the challenge.[8] Defoe still had to spend time defending his uncertain command of Latin against those who, whether they had gone to Oxbridge or not, lampooned the fluency of the 'hosier'.

What we do know is that Daniel courted Mary Tuffley, the daughter of the wealthy cooper John Tuffley of Aldgate. Since so many goods were transported in casks and barrels, expert coopers were, like tallow chandlers, able to amass considerable fortunes, and by the time Daniel was stepping out with Mary, Tuffley owned appreciable property in London and Surrey. When they married in January 1684 Mary's dowry was £3,700 (£750,000 in today's values on a calculation of average inflation), making her new household in Cornhill exceptionally affluent. Again, we need not quiz ourselves too much over the marriage of two children of successful merchants from the same neighbourhood, but it is telling that in 1683 Daniel wooed Mary with a collection of copied stories, *Historical Collections*, in which, according to Maximillian Novak, 'too large a number involved tales of great gestures by leaders of nations or of heroism in battle to suggest that the young Defoe was ready for the contemplative life'.[9] In the *Review* and elsewhere Defoe makes occasional reference to his sword, and, of course, Crusoe was extraordinarily well armed. All of which indicates that Daniel was not cut out as a clergyman, but it may also give a hint as to why even a man who would develop into an inveterate risk-taker made the extraordinary decision in June 1685 to join the rebellion of the Duke of Monmouth, Charles II's illegitimate Protestant son, when he had been married for less than two years and had just started a family.

It may well have been the speedy resolution of James II, who became king on 6 February 1685, to uphold and even extend his brother's absolutism, in bypassing parliament, fixing elections against the Whigs, and prosecuting Presbyterian clergy that persuaded Defoe and other young Dissenters of his generation to resort to armed insurrection. Monmouth had been a hero of the wars against the Dutch, but when he landed at Lyme Regis on 11 June with eighty-two men, he had fewer than would accompany Fidel Castro on the *Granma* in 1956. Moreover, for nearly a month the government had been enforcing general warrants for the search of 'Traytors and conspirators', and upon news of Monmouth's landing fifty-eight named individuals, most of them prominent Nonconformists, were ordered to be detained, a total of some two hundred eventually being arrested. The River Thames, with just one bridge, was readily invigilated, and London's dozen approach roads were mainly controlled to the northeast with detachments of James's army at Stratford, Highgate, Islington, and Bow. Yet despite this, Monmouth's army eventually grew to three thousand, so control was not complete and some, probably including Defoe, had left before the crackdown.

They were, however, heading for disaster. Monmouth's largely untrained troops were obliged to undertake long marches in poor weather and the demanding terrain of the West Country. On 6 July in an ill-advised effort to launch a night attack on the king's well-prepared forces, they were betrayed by a stray shot, caught by cannon fire in marshland, and then chased down in full-flight by royal dragoons. Perhaps two-thirds of the rebels escaped the battlefield at Sedgemoor, but so comprehensive was the defeat that most of them were captured over the next two weeks. Only those on horseback and with a plausible excuse to be travelling in Somerset, Dorset, or Devon were able to evade capture. Amongst that group of perhaps four hundred was Daniel Defoe, for whom we have no judicial record beyond his eventual pardon of 1687 (for which he probably paid £60). It has sensibly been suggested that the rebel cavalry never properly engaged in the fight because their untrained horses had been spooked by the sound of gunfire. Thereafter Defoe may well have been able to show that he had been in the region on business.[10] He never came to trial on account of involvement in the rebellion. Monmouth, who was defeated by John Churchill, the future Duke of Marlborough, alongside whom he had fought in Europe, was taken to London and subjected to a gruesomely incompetent beheading.

Many, of course, did not have Daniel Defoe's luck, as they were caught up in what became known as the Bloody Assizes under Judge George Jeffreys. Following the king's early demand for exemplary punishment, Jeffreys presided over the execution of two hundred fifty men in six towns in less than a month. It is then that Benjamin Hewlings and the other young Londoners were killed. There are very few surviving transcripts of any due process that may be claimed to have occurred in the trials, and subsequently there was a concerted Whig campaign of commemoration, as in *The New Martyrology, or the Bloody Assizes* (January 1689), which contained many scaffold speeches. But many must have been invented by John Tutchin, who himself cannot be shown by any tangible evidence to have pleaded for execution in lieu of the sentence of seven years' gaol and annual flogging in every market town of Devon. The beheading of Dame Alice Lisle of Ringwood, Hampshire, for harbouring two fugitives, apparently the last instance of a woman being judicially beheaded in England, was particularly infamous. But it was also, as Melinda Zook explains, exceptional, as it did not conform to the full punishment for high treason:

> Rebels were hanged until unconscious, disembowelled, beheaded and quartered. Their remains were then boiled in brine, covered in black tar and set up on poles and lampposts. Residents and

visitors found the sight of the exhibited body parts frightening and the smell nauseating. Only after a progress through the west the following year did James II himself, disturbed by what he saw, order the heads and quarters to be removed and buried.[11]

Such barbarism, of course, conforms to Foucault's contrast with a subsequent socialisation of discipline and obedience. However, treason remained apart from other capital crimes, which, as E.P. Thompson and others have shown, increased throughout the eighteenth century and were by no means the exclusive caprice of absolutist monarchs. Domestic servants who stole from their employers were liable to execution, and, as Warden of the Mint, Isaac Newton ordered at least a dozen executions of clippers and counterfeiters following the recoinage of 1696. The Transportation Act of 1718 allowed for an alternative to execution, but dismembered corpses of traitors were exhibited on Temple Bar as late as 1723.[12]

Hier komen de hollandse soldaten

On 22 October 1685, just weeks after Sedgemoor, King Louis XIV of France revoked the Edict of Nantes under which French Protestants had received the right to practice their religion without persecution for nearly a century. Churches and schools were now destroyed with official licence as they had been in fact under the *dragonnades* encouraged by the crown since 1681. Hundreds of thousands of Huguenots fled the country over the following years, many of them settling in the east of London, close to the City, where Daniel Defoe lived. Louis XIV was a cousin of James II and had subsidised Charles II. Dynastic, religious, and international politics were fusing fiercely. A key further element in this combustible equation was the fact that James's older daughter Mary, a Protestant, was married to another cousin, William of Orange, the stadtholder of the Dutch Republic since 1672 and a staunch Calvinist.

The overseas dimension of the escalating conflict was emphasised by James's increased reliance on Richard Talbot, First Earl of Tyrconnell, the first Catholic to serve as Lord Deputy of Ireland for over one hundred fifty years and active supporter of the king's transfer of Irish soldiers to England. As Catholic officers started to arrive in English camps in the summer of 1688, English troops began to whistle the Irish jig that had begun life as 'An Antidote Against Melancholy' but now took on the title of 'Lillibulero' and would acquire pungently political lyrics when William accepted the invitation from English dignitaries to invade so that Mary might replace James as monarch. William's landing at Torbay on 5 November 1688 opened what soon became known as the 'Glorious Revolution', at the military heart of which were Dutch troops who only a decade earlier had been fighting against the English. The immediate conflict was interrupted when James fled to France in December 1688, but he sought to reconquer England and Scotland from Ireland the following year, only to be defeated by William's army at the Battle of the Boyne in July 1690.

The Boyne ended the military phase of the Revolution in the British Isles, but it was only one early engagement in the Nine Years War between France and an alliance of England, the Dutch Republic, Spain, and the Holy Roman Empire. That conflict lasted until 1697 and was followed by the War of Spanish Succession of 1701–1713, with Great Britain again ranged with various allies against France. For over twenty years both wars were conducted on an international scale, on land and on sea, having considerable financial consequences and, arguably, even greater ones for merchants reliant upon international trade, such as Daniel Defoe.

Perhaps the peak of Defoe's public life was reached on 29 October 1689, when he formed part of the official 'military' reception for William and Mary at a magnificent banquet at the Guildhall, just streets away from his home. He was now a Freeman of the City of London, and so effectively part of local government as well as a respected citizen. His first child, Mary, had died a year before, and his eighth born in 1701 would also die in infancy, but the others formed part of that two-thirds of the population that made it to their fifteenth birthday. At no stage does Defoe write ill of his wife, and on occasion he praised her fulsomely with good reason, as we will see. But there is no doubt that within a decade of the marriage he embarrassed her acutely as well as putting the family's safety at risk because on 29 October 1692—exactly three years after the Guildhall reception—Defoe was committed to the Fleet prison for bankruptcy.

Part of that unpaid debt dated back to mid-1688 and involved the loss of one ship, *Desire*, to French privateers after England had declared war, whilst the master of another craft failed to accumulate sufficient cargo and passengers promised from Defoe's factors in Boston and Maryland. Suit and counter-suit kept these matters on the boil, and it seems that Defoe had not assiduously insured his voyage with the buoyant maritime undertakers led by Edward Lloyd. But then things started to get really strange. In

October 1691, one Joseph Williams patented a diving bell that he had been testing off the Scottish coast. Defoe spent £200 on ten shares and joined the new company as its secretary. But the bell failed, the capital was lost. (Defoe—rather like Jules Verne—didn't lose interest in submarine enterprises; his brother-in-law Robert Davis descended in a bell in September 1704, singing Psalm 100 to Daniel's reported approval.)[13]

In April 1692 Defoe agreed a price of £852.15 with John Barksdale for the purchase of a civet cat farm with seventy animals in Stoke Newington. Civets, native to Africa and Asia, secrete a soft, pale yellow substance from a pouch just above the anus that, when diluted, changes from a putrid to a sweet aroma, used to create perfume. The extraction of the oil is not easy, requiring a narrow cage and an expertly applied spatula once a week, but the rewards promised to be considerable. The problem, however, was that Defoe had borrowed heavily—including £800 from Mary's mother Joan Tuffley—to make the purchase and then sustain ownership once this came into question. After a string of resales and effective subleases, the sheriffs eventually seized the installation, which was shown to be half the value he had 'paid' for. The reason why his mother-in-law, whose servants had maintained the farm for months, became one of the plaintiffs against Daniel is obscure and controversial, but they did not subsequently become estranged, even though the farm and the cash were lost.[14]

By October Defoe had amassed debts of £17,000 (approximately £3.9 million in 2018 terms) from one hundred forty creditors, all but four of whom accepted his offer of 15 shillings to the pound. However, the four, holding debts of £2,000 refused that deal, occasioning Daniel's detention in the Fleet and then the King's Bench prison. He did not serve a prolonged sentence but was in and out of court and jail for the next year. He had been 'broken'. In purely financial terms, Defoe would recover, but the experience of bankruptcy had been so traumatic that it reappeared many times in his writing on economic and commercial matters. It is at this time that he drafted *An Essay Upon Projects,* eventually published in 1697, when identifying the lived experience between the written lines might have been a touch more difficult:

> There are . . . too many, fair pretences of fine discoveries, new inventions, engines, and I know not what, which—being advanced in notion, and talked up to great things to be performed when such and such sums of money shall be advanced, and such and such engines are made—have raised the fancies of credulous people to such a height that, merely on the shadow of expectation, they have formed companies, chose committees, appointed officers, shares, and books, raised great stocks, and cried up an empty notion . . .[15]

This was more than twenty years before the South Sea Bubble, but that experience undoubtedly sharpened his fear of bankruptcy:

> Breaking is the death of a Tradesman; he is mortally stabb'd, or, as we may say, shot through the head in his trading capacity; his shop is shut up, as it is when a man is buried; his credit the life blood of his trade, is stagnated; and his attendance, which was the pulse of his business, is stop't, and beats no more . . .[16]

No wonder that elsewhere in *The Compleat English Tradesman* (II, 1727) Defoe observes that

> A Tradesman is never safe; his condition is subject to innumerable casualties, and to unavoidable disaster. No estate is so big as not to be in hazard, no posture of his affairs out of the reach of accidents. While he continues in trade, like a seaman, though he is at the mouth of the harbour, nay, safe in port, and come to an anchor, he can never say he is entirely out of danger, and perfectly safe, till he has set both feet on shore.[17]

Bankruptcy, in short, is a shipwreck.

It is unsurprising that Marx quoted Defoe's writing on credit, for throughout his life he returned to it as a core component not just of the rapidly evolving mercantile system but also of its civic underpinning:

> The credit of a tradesman consists in his punctual payment of his bills, and demands of every kind, and this credit may be untainted and spotless as to trade, when he may have no reputation, as a man of worth, a man of value, or as to his morals, or his personal and relative conduct in his neighbourhood.[18]

And yet there is a perilous paradox in this source of respectability and commercial survival, for Lady Credit

> Is a coy Lass, and wonderful chary of her self . . . If once she be disoblig'd, she's the most difficult to be Friends again with us,

and yet she will court those most, who have no occacion for her; and will stand at their Doors neglected and ill-us'd, scorn'd, and rejected, like a Beggar, and never leave them . . . If you court her, you lose her, or must buy her at unreasonable Rates; and if you do, she is always jealous of you, and Suspicious . . .[19]

This is a worldly condition. Yet, as in *Crusoe*, Providence still prevails: 'Christianity supposes we acknowledge that life and all the contingencies of life are subjected to the dominion of Providence'. As Sandra Sherman comments,

Defoe has it both ways. One can be Christian and pragmatic, erasing the immorality of non-performance because the market and God operate beyond our control (let alone ability to predict). Under such a rationale, it is absurd, even blasphemous, to require that a man pull back from the market to a place where promises are sure.[20]

The Price of Virtue

For the historian J.G.A. Pocock the emergence of this world of borrowing and lending marked the eclipse of another era, which he termed 'The Machiavellian Moment', when humanist values of civility had related to the possession of land that 'provided the individual with power, leisure, and independence'. That in turn permitted the landowner to be an active citizen, 'virtuous in his devotion to the public good' and as 'farmer-warrior' virtuous also in his autonomy from

> any relation which might render him corrupt . . . Property was both an extension and a prerequisite of personality . . . He did not possess it in order to engage in trade, exchange or profit; indeed, these activities were hardly compatible with the activity of citizenship.[21]

Of course, in 1700, the landed interest remained exceptionally powerful, not just in terms of rural hierarchy and the influence of the Church, but also in the Commons, where it was strongly represented by the Tory party.

> No Court or Whig writer, neither Defoe nor Addison, ever dreamed of denying that land was substantially what its partisans said it was. They could indeed argue that land was of no value, even in rendering its proprietor independent, without money and trade, and there was a line of rhetoric which suggested that a society with no wealth but its land—Gothic England, contemporary Poland, or the Scottish Highlands—would lack both liberty (the tenants being subject to their lords) and culture.[22]

In this new world of mobile property, where wealth was by definition not finite, traditional values may not have been comprehensively displaced but they inevitably came under challenge. For Defoe, we will recall, 'I divide the care and concern of the nation among these generals, religion, constitution and commerce. Trade I rank with religion and constitution.' In an equally Whig vein, he saw the health of such trade in it being expansionist and international:

> Improving and extending our colonies in America, Africa and Muscovy, in order to increase the consumption of our manufactures, and secure an employ to our people, let the accidents of war be what they will. [23]

However, party lines were quite fluid in the decades after the Revolution, with both Whigs and Tories fractured over religion and foreign policy in particular. For Pocock, Defoe's early place on the modern wing of whiggism placed him at odds with the classical republican strand of the movement that derived many of its ideas from James Harrington's *The Commonwealth of Oceana* (1656) and looked back to a moment closer in time than Machiavelli's Florentine republic but scarcely less rooted in the morality of individuality. Pocock is reluctant to generalise beyond the 'Anglosphere' of the North Atlantic world, but there he ventures a quite conclusive interpretation:

> Defoe asserted that a society built on military service and tenure was not only feudal but baronial, uncultivated, violent, and repressive; true freedom was modern and could only be found in commercial society, where the individual might profit by wealth and enlightenment and did not risk his liberty in paying others to defend and govern him, so long as he retained parliamentary control of the purse strings . . . The old Whigs identified freedom with virtue and located it in the past; the Modern Whigs

identified it with wealth, enlightenment and progress toward a
future. Around this synthesis, it is not too much to say, nearly all
eighteenth-century philosophy of history can be organized . . .[24]

Aside from commerce and religion, the new virtue lay within the constitutional order also identified by Defoe as a 'general', and whilst he shifted
in his relative attitude to monarch, parliament, and the crowd, he never
vacillated in seeing them as tightly interdependent.

He served as a juror and in other local offices, both in Cornhill and
Stoke Newington, but Defoe never sought election as an MP to promote
his vision of modernity. This is fully visible in *An Essay Upon Projects,* which
brims with radical ideas for public policy, including a fiscal proposal some
two hundred years before its time:

> In a general tax . . . it should be the poor, who are not able to
> pay . . . a poor labourer, who works for twelve pence or eighteen
> pence a day, does not drink a pot of beer but pays the king a tenth
> part for excise; and really pays more to the king's taxes in a year
> than a country shopkeeper, who is alderman of the town, worth
> perhaps two or three thousand pounds, brews his own beer, pays
> no excise, and in the land-tax is rated it may be at £100, and pays
> £1.4s. per annum, but ought, if the Act were put into execution,
> to pay £36 per annum to the king.[25]

Other, rather less redistributionist proposals included the establishment
of banks in England's fifteen main towns; the construction of sixty-seven

'high post-roads', one hundred forty miles of 'cross-roads' and a thousand miles of 'bye-lanes and passes', all ditched, drained, and repaired at an estimated cost of £263,040; a variable system of assurances according to profession, but including seamen, 'the forlorn hope of the world', who would receive £25 for the loss of an eye and £50 for the loss of one leg; a widows' pension fund; a lottery for charity; academies for young women ('we reproach the sex every day with folly and impertinence, while I am confident, had they the advantages of education equal to us, they would be guilty of less than ourselves'); and, quite predictably, a detailed reform of the bankruptcy laws, based on the distinction between the honest debtor, 'the knavish, designing, or idle extravagant debtor', the moderate creditor who 'will hear reasonable, and just arguments', and 'the rigorous, severe creditor who 'will have his debt . . . without mercy, without compassion'.

One of the more notable features of this publication was its invective against swearing, which, of course, meant a great deal more in a truly God-fearing society than today:

> 'Tis a senseless, foolish, ridiculous Practice; 'tis a Mean to manner of End; 'tis Words spoken which signify nothing; 'tis Folly acted for the sake of Folly, which is something even the Devil himself don't practice: The Devil does evil, we say, but it is for some design, either to seduce others, or, as some Divines say, from a Principle of Emnity to his Maker: Men Steal for Gain, and Murther to gratify their Avarice or Revenge; Whoredoms and Ravishments, Adulteries and Sodomy, are committed to please a

vicious Appetite, and have always alluring Objects; and generally all Vices have some previous Cause, and some visible Tendency; but this, of all Vicious Practices, seems the most Nonsensical and Ridiculous; there is neither Pleasure nor Profit; no Design pursued, no Lust gratified, but it is a mere Frenzy of the Tongue, a Vomit of the Brain, which works by putting a Contrary upon the Course of Nature.[26]

This concern with the way of words was matched by an interest in crime (and punishment) that would re-emerge as a central theme in *Moll Flanders* and *Roxana* and the pirate works.

A few days after the appearance of *An Essay Upon Projects* Defoe issued a much more politically critical pamphlet, *The Poor Man's Plea*, arguing that the letter of the law with regard to profanity, drunkenness, and lewdness was unobjectionable, but the power and practice of the upper classes were such that they were always treated more leniently than the poor man:

These are all cobweb laws in which the small flies are catched, and the great ones break through. My Lord Mayor has whipt about the poor beggars, and a few scandalous whores have been sent to the House of Correction; some alehousekeepers and vintners have been fined for drawing drink on the Sabbath-day; but all of this falls on us of the mob, the poor plebeii, as if all the vice lay among us; for we do not find the rich drunkard carried before my Lord Mayor, not a swearing lewd merchant fined, or set in the stocks. The man with the gold ring and gay cloths may swear before the

Justice, or at the Justice; may reel home through the open streets, and no man take any notice of it; but if a poor man get drunk, or swear an oath, he must take to the stocks without remedy.

Defoe completes this invective with an attack on blasphemous and hypocritical magistrates who 'shall punish a man for drunkenness, with a God *damn him, set him in the stocks*'.[27] A decade later London's Societies for the Reformation of Manners were initiating prosecutions of an order to suggest that the new ideology of 'politeness' was simply skimming the surface: swearing and cursing 626; Sabbath-breaking 1,187; drunkenness 150; lewd and disorderly 1,255; keeping a bawdy house 51; gaming 30.[28] Undeterred, Defoe declared later in life, 'My Satyr shall in quiet sleep, while Parsons cease to drink and whore . . . While Lawyers cease to talk Mankind to Death . . . While C[ourtier]s Promises regard.'[29]

*

Even though the Whigs and independents held a clear majority in the House of Commons when Defoe's pamphlets appeared, there was precious little chance of his ideas even being debated, let alone adopted. Nonetheless, their mere emergence reflected the significant loosening of liberties since the Revolution, most especially with the Toleration Act of 1689, which rescinded much of Clarendon's penal code although it purposefully did not apply to Roman Catholics, Quakers, atheists, and Unitarians (whose public worship remained proscribed until 1813). Moreover, Occasional Conformity was still required for those who wished to hold public office. Still, in its first year nearly 800 temporary and 143 permanent Nonconformist meeting places were established. By 1710 there were 2,500.[30]

The Stuarts had effectively treated the House of Commons as an enemy. Between 1679 and 1688 the House met just five times, for a total of 171 days; from 1689 to 1698 it met eleven times, for a total of 1,300 days. Under the entire Restoration era Parliament passed 564 statutes; from the accession of William and Mary (1689) to that of George I (1714) 2,550 laws were passed. The pace of politics accelerated after the 1694 Triennial act which mandated general elections every three years, so that fifteen were held between 1689 and 1717 although the Septennial Act of 1716 increased the maximum period between polls to seven years. Moreover, the political nation understood as the electorate, was small. In the counties it was restricted to those who held freehold property worth 40 shillings a year, whereas the franchise in the boroughs varied considerably, from any lodger in Taunton to full church and local taxpayers in Berkshire's four parliamentary boroughs. Julian Hoppit reckons that in 1700 there were some 118,000 electors in the counties, each of which returned two MPs, and 70,000 in the boroughs, many of which were 'rotten' and did not hold meaningful contests.[31] All the same, the Commons now mattered hugely to the conduct of policy, and its principal power was that which Daniel Defoe deemed vital to the constitution—control over money ('supply').

Equally, the formation of the Bank of England in 1694 (as a private institution) enabled a permanent national debt to be established, lending the treasury £1.2 million that year to bolster the issue in 1693 of £1 million in annuities at a very substantial 14 per cent (double the maximum allowed for private debts). This emergence of a market in securities provided a new source of 'virtue' in lending to the government by buying its bonds so that it might provide security. In the mid-1690s, at a time of warfare and with William striving to consolidate his reign after Mary's death in 1694, these innovations did not yet amount to the 'Financial Revolution' that historians would later identify. Additional revenue was found in new taxes on hackney carriages (1694), houses (1696), and hawkers (1697). Just as importantly, the clipping of coin had reached such a stage—perhaps 70 per cent of all coins in circulation at a loss of bullion of £703,000 in 1694—that John Locke supported, and Isaac Newton implemented, a major recoinage in 1696, with the face value of coins being very expensively matched by their intrinsic value.[32] New minting technology greatly reduced the problem, but, of course, those on low wages still needed credit from stores and taverns—one reason why Defoe consistently argued for a high wage economy. As a dealer in wines and brandies, he was very familiar on the excise regime, which in these cases had to be enforced in the face of challenges from smugglers, privateers, and outright pirates. In the case of beer, mentioned by Defoe in *An Essay Upon Projects,* home production was extensive, and general consumption at over fifty gallons (strong and small beer) per head in 1689 suggests an eminently taxable habit as well as the dangers of the urban water supply.[33]

These changes were driven by warfare. The navy was exceptionally expensive, accounting for nearly half of military expenditure in the 1690s, with the number of sailors doubling to nearly fifty thousand and the dockyard labour force to nearly six thousand at the end of the War of Spanish Succession in 1713. The army rose to some ninety thousand troops, with perhaps 15 per cent of the male labour force serving in the armed forces. Hoppit describes an effective 'militarisation' of society that cost the state £4.9 million a year in the 1690s and £7.8 million in the War of Spanish Succession.[34] The government's debt, which had been zero at the accession of William and Mary rose to £36 million at the Peace of Utrecht in 1713.

As a merchant Daniel Defoe had to contend with the commercial consequences on a daily basis, but he also engaged with policy and political controversies as a writer, first on his own account, and later as a journalist supporting the government. In 1698 he waded into a debate that had divided Whigs as well as raising Tory objections to the maintenance of the army after the Treaty of Ryswick the previous year. In *An Argument shewing that a Standing Army, with Consent of Parliament, is not inconsistent with a Free Government* Defoe rebutted both those who argued for the complete standdown of regular forces, to be replaced by a citizen militia, and those who failed to understand the fears engendered from past military domination:

> Some People talk so big of our own Strength, that they think England able to Defend it self against all the World. I presume such talk without Book; I think the prudentest Course is to prevent the Trial, and that is only to hold the Balance of Europe as the King now does; and if there be a War to keep it abroad. How these Gentlemen will do that with a Militia, I should be glad to see Propos'd . . . But the Parliament we see needs no Instructions in this Matter, and therefore are providing to reduce the Forces to the same Quota they were in before 1680, by which means all the

fear of Invading our Liberties will be at an end, the Army being
so very small that 'tis impossible.[35]

The outbreak of the War of Spanish Succession within four years meant
that the reduction did not last very long. On the other hand, the war was
indeed fought abroad, and now in such large formations—multinational
armies of one hundred thousand commonly took the field—and with suffi-
cient developments in technology, particularly the widespread replacement
of the matchlock with the flintlock musket, that the existence of a standing
army ceased to be controversial. The debate now moved on to whether
the navy should shoulder the bulk of operations, as the Tories favoured,
and whether the strategy undertaken by the Duke of Marlborough—prolonged manoeuvre, aversion of joining battle on sub-optimal terms—was
sustainable.

Defoe's interest in the balance of power had its own logic, but it also
stemmed from his attention to the international defence of Protestantism
and his almost fervent admiration for William III. As with the issue of a
standing army, this set him against not only hard-line ('nonjuring') Tories,
whether or not they supported the Jacobite cause, but also that faction of
Whigs who felt that too much power was concentrated in the court and
disliked the retention of Dutch guards. Prominent amongst these was the
same John Tutchin who had suffered after Sedgemoor, assembled *The New
Martyrology,* and now aimed at the promotion by William of his Dutch
friends—particularly Hans Willem Bentinck, the Earl of Portland—to the
English nobility in a xenophobic doggerel *The Foreigners:*[36]

These are the Vermin do our State molest:

Eclipse our Glory, and disturb our Rest.

BENTIR in the Inglorious Roll the first,

Bentir to this and future Ages curst,

Of mean Descent, yet insolently proud,

Shunn'd by the Great, and hated by the Crowd;

Who neither Blood nor Parentage can boast,

And what he got the *Jewish* Nation lost . . .

Defoe declared himself 'filled with a kind of rage', and in January 1701 published (anonymously) a riposte in what is surely his best poem, *The True-Born Englishman: A Satyr*.

As was often the case, he began this work with a condensed preface:

. . . the Intent of the Satyr is pointed at the Vanity of those who talk of their Antiquity, and value themselves upon their Pedigree, their Ancient Families, and being *True Born*; whereas 'tis impossible that we shou'd be *True Born*; and if we could, shou'd have lost by the bargain.

But then he let go with a massive 1,250-line poem, opening with mockery of national characterisations and their underlying prejudices: Spain too proud to be rich; Italy full of lust, drunken Germany; and fickle, dancing France, and so on.[37] But Defoe spends most of his time on the origins of his own generation of English:

DANIEL DEFOE

. . . .The *Romans* first with *Julius Caesar*, came,
Including all the Nations of that Name,
Gauls, *Greeks*, and *Lombards*; and by Computation,
Auxiliaries or Slaves of ev'ry Nation.
With *Hengist*, *Saxons*; *Danes* with Sueno came,
In search of Plunder, not in search of Fame.
Scots, *Picts*, and *Irish* from th' *Hibernian* Shore:
And Conqu'ring *William* brought the *Normans* o're

All these their Barb'rous Offspring left behind,
The Dregs of Armies, they of all Mankind:
Blended with *Britains* who before were here,
Of whom the *Welsh* ha' blest the Character.

From this Amphibious Ill-born Mob began
That vain ill-natur'd thing, an Englishman.
The Customs, Sirnames, Languages and Manners,
Of all these Nations are their own Explainers:
Whose Relicks are so lasting and so Strong,
They ha' left a *Shiboleth* upon our Tongue;
By which with easy search you may distinguish
Your *Roman-Saxon-Danish-Norman* English.

. . . These are the Heroes that despise the *Dutch*,
And rail at new-come Foreigners so much;
Forgetting that themselves are all deriv'd

From the most Scoundrel Race that ever liv'd.

A horrid Medly of Thieves and Drones,

Who ransack'd Kingdoms, and dispeopl'd Towns.

The *Pict* and Painted *Britain*, Treach'rous *Scot*,

By Hunger, Theft, and Rapine, hither brought.

Norwegian Pirates, Buccaneering *Danes*,

Whose Red-hair'd Offspring ev'ry where remains.

Who join'd with *Norman-French*, compound the Breed

From whence your *True-Born Englishmen* proceed.

The poem was an immediate success, and it continued to be so after William's death, fifty editions being printed by mid-century. Defoe claimed that the King had personally favoured him for the work, and he would sometimes remove the cover of anonymity, styling himself 'The Author of *The True-Born Englishman*'. Even those who despised his prolixity, lack of gentility, and whiggish convictions recognised its power, which stands up pretty well in the age of UKIP, the DUP, and Brexit. John Tutchin, by contrast, did poorly. His Cromwellian instincts and distempered, often unsourced, accusations of corruption got him arrested and forced to flee to enemy France. Upon his return, failing to modulate his behaviour in a manner now well learned by Defoe, in 1707 Tutchin accused the Royal Navy of secretly supplying food to their French foes (a practice of the Dutch, who did not see war as reason enough to suspend trade, whereas blockade was viewed by both the British and the French as an integral part of grand strategy). Marlborough was infuriated, and Tutchin again jailed, where he died after a severe beating by unidentified aggressors.

Despite currying favour with the monarch Daniel Defoe had been very lucky not to suffer a similar fate because, probably boosted by the renown of his great poem, in May 1701 he embarked upon openly activist politics, against the House of Commons, which refused to fund the military in a manner that he had advocated precisely on the condition of Parliament's guarantee. The issue had extended beyond the confines of Westminster when, in late April, five representatives of the freeholders of Kent presented a petition to the Commons, urging immediate action—'that our religion and safety may be effectually provided for'—in view of the county's plain vulnerability to a French invasion. Although the Tories had not gained a landslide victory in the elections of January as a result of post-war decline in Whig popularity, they held a working majority, and, suspecting some Whig manoeuvre, ordered the petitioners to be arrested. Two weeks later Defoe, 'guarded by about sixteen men of quality', presented the Speaker, Robert Harley, what became known as *Legion's Memorial*. This document did not beat about the bush from the very start:

Begin: Mr S[peake]r.

The inclosed Memorial you are charged with, in the Behalf of many Thousands of the good People of England.

There is neither Popish, Jacobite, Seditious, or Party Interest concern'd in it; but Honesty and Truth.

You are commanded by Two Hundred Thousand Englishmen, to deliver it to the H[ous]e of C[ommon]s, and to inform them that it is no Banter, but serious Truth; and a serious Regard to it is expected; nothing but Justice, and their Duty is required, and it is required by them who have both a Right to require, and Power to compel, viz. the People of England . . .

As if this were not clear enough, the *Memorial* expressly restated the right of popular resistance against oppressive rule:

If the maladministration of governors [has] extended to tyranny and oppression, to destruction of right and justice, overthrowing the constitution, and abusing the people, the people have thought it lawful to reassume the right of government into their own hands, to reduce their governors to reason.[38]

This blunt assertion of a people's authority over its parliamentary representatives took some courage to present, even if Defoe was disguised as a woman, as his enemies later claimed. In any event, if it was indeed the first time Defoe and Harley met, this was scarcely a propitious encounter as the Speaker, who also came from a dissenting background but had shifted to a moderate toryism, would shortly become a senior figure in the government. Danger, though, was averted. The petition was delivered, and when the Commons rose on 24 June, having eventually enhanced the military budget, the initial petitioners were released to popular acclaim. Daniel

Defoe's radical star could scarcely be higher, and he was also favoured by an active monarch aged 52. What could possibly go wrong?

Big Mistake

Early in 1702, with England entering a new war, King William fell from his horse, Sorrel, at Hampton Court when the mount tripped over a molehill. His broken shoulder was set without difficulty, but he contracted pneumonia and died on 8 March. William was succeeded by his sister-in-law Anne, who was English and who made a point in her first speech from the throne in May of her firm adherence to 'the interests and religion of the Church of England' and that her principles 'will incline me to countenance those who have the truest zeal to support it'.[39] This was taken as a signal for a muscular reassertion of High Church values, Tory ascendency—confirmed in their control of Commons after the July election, with 298 seats, against 184 for the Whigs—and a new, pugnacious offensive against Occasional Conformity.

Defoe himself had serious issues with Occasional Conformity, writing that it was tantamount to '*playing-Bopeep* with God Almighty'.[40] But this may have more public face than inner conviction since in the years since his bankruptcy he himself had taken up posts—overseeing the accounts of the tax on glassware, 1695–99, at £100 a year, and serving as a trustee of a lottery—that would, under normal circumstances, have required some conspicuous observation of the rites of the Church of England. He seemed in practice, if not in rhetoric, to be moving into the mainstream. In the 1690s he had acquired a property at Tilbury on the Thames estuary, where he had established a tile- and brick-manufacturing plant that he claimed was clearing £600 a year in profit and employed one hundred families. In 1696, Greenwich Hospital bought 162,500 bricks from him, so he might well be thought to be enjoying the sort of underlying confidence that underpinned *An Essay Upon Projects*.[41] Moreover, he was succeeding in cancelling most of his debts and getting generally favourable judgements from the courts when these were contested. It was the war of words that provoked Daniel Defoe back into the danger-zone.

On 31 May 1702, Dr. Henry Sacheverell, a twenty-eight-year-old High Church fellow of Magdalen College Oxford, preached a sermon entitled *The Political Union* at the University Church of St. Mary the Virgin in which he insisted in aggressive language upon the union of church and state, denigrating Dissenters, occasional conformists, and their Whig supporters. In this heartland of toryism, Sacheverell urged Anglicans not 'to strike sail to a party which is an open and avowed enemy to our communion', but rather to 'hang out the bloody flag and banner of defiance':

> If therefore We have any Concern for our *Religion,* any True Allegiance for Our *Sovereign* or Regard to the Safety and Honour of Our *Country*, We must Watch against these Crafty, Faithless, and Insidious Persons, who can *Creep* to Our Altars, and Partake of Our Sacraments, that They may be *Qualify'd*, more Secretly and Powerfully to Undermine Us.[42]

Astonishing a later congregation with 'the fiery red that over-spread his face . . . and the goggling wildness of his eyes', the 'Bloody Flag Officer' had set a new order of invective in a forty-year controversy.[43]

Daniel Defoe was provoked. His poetic satyr had worked wonderfully well, and he had just issued an attack on the principle of 'passive obedience' (that it is never legitimate to resist a lawful king, however unjust and tyrannical) that Sacheverell so supported. Why not follow it up with a mock High Church sermon that took Sacheverell's delivery to its logical conclusion? *The Shortest-Way with the Dissenters; or Proposals for the Establishment of the Church* was issued at the end of the year, with Defoe's mimicry in full cry:

> And now they find their Day is over, their Power gone, and the Throne of this Nation possest by a Royal, *English*, True and ever Constant Member of, and Friend to the Church of *England* . . . . now they cry out *Peace, Union, Forbearance*, and *Charity*, as if the Church had not too long harbour'd her Enemies under her Wing, and nourish'd the viperous brood, till they hiss and fly in the Face of the Mother that cherish'd them . . .

> The Representatives of the Nation have now an Opportunity, the Time is come when all good Men ha' wish'd for, that the Gentlemen of *England* may serve the Church of *England; now they are protected and encouraged by a Church of* England *Queen.*
> *What will ye do for your Sister in the Day that she shall be spoken for.*
> If ever you will establish the best Christian Church in the World.
> If ever you will suppress the Spirit of Enthusiasm.

If ever you will free the Nation from the viperous Brood that have so long suck'd the Blood of their Mother . . .

Now *let us Crucifie the Thieves*. Let her Foundations be establish'd upon the Destruction of her Enemies: The Doors of Mercy being always open to the returning Part of the Deluded People; let the Obstinate be rul'd with the Road of Iron.[44]

These words, published nearly a decade after the 1695 Licensing Act, which had lifted prior censorship, deceived and enthralled some Tories, but Defoe had gambled hugely, especially by including so many references to Queen Anne. The polemic was anonymous, but his authorship was announced in the *Observator* by none other than John Tutchin, who reaped sweet revenge for *The True-Born Englishman*. Defoe had miscalculated not just in his judgement of the allowable limits of rhetoric but also in the fact that he had previously enjoyed the support of William and some Whig grandees. Now he was on his own. He went on the run, possibly to Holland, but more likely in London, amongst the Whig and Dissenting underground.

A week after Tutchin had grassed him up, the government's *London Gazette* announced a £50 reward for information leading to the capture of 'Daniel de Fooe', who was the author of a 'Scandalous and Seditious' publication:

He is a middle Sized Spare Man about 40 years old, of a brown Complexion, and dark brown coloured Hair wears a Wig, a hooked Nose, a sharp Chin, grey Eyes, and a large Mould near

his Mouth, was born in *London*, and for many years was a Hose
Factor in Freeman's-yard, in Corn hill, and is now Owner of the
brick and Pantile Works near *Tilbury-Fort in Essex.*[45]

It was clear that chickens were coming home to roost when Robert Harley,
the put-upon Speaker of the Commons, persuaded the government to begin
an investigation, which was led by Daniel Finch, the Earl of Nottingham,
whose lugubrious demeanour had earned him the nickname 'Dismal'.
Nottingham knew well enough how to proceed, detaining Edward Bellamy,
a Whig agent, and George Croome, the printer of the pamphlet, and order-
ing Defoe's arrest and the seizure of his papers and books. Eventually the
House of Commons and the Old Bailey laid rather different charges against
him, but both treated Defoe's depiction of the monarchy as seditious:

> De Foe . . . being a Seditious man and of a disordered mind, and a
> person of bad name, reputation and Conversation, by a disgrace-
> ful felony perfidiously, mischievously and seditiously contriving,
> practicing and purposing to make and Cause discord between . . .
> the Queen and her . . . Subjects, and to Disunite and set at vari-
> ance the Protestant Subjects of . . . the Queen and to alarm All her
> Protestant Subjects Dissenting from the Church of England . . .[46]

The clandestine author first sought in a further pamphlet, *A Brief Explanation
of a Late Pamphlet,* to persuade the government in as conciliatory tone as
he could contrive that he had simply sought to perform a public service
through the exaggerated use of language to show the High Tories,

That 'tis Nonsense to go round about, and tell us of the Crimes of the Dissenters, to prepare the World to believe they are not fit to Live in a Humane Society, that they are Enemies to the Government, and Law, to the Queen, and the Public Peace, and the like; the *shortest way*, and the soonest, wou'd be to tell us plainly that they wou'd have them all Hang'd, Banish'd and Destroyed.[47]

He was digging himself deeper into the hole.

Defoe stayed in hiding, but in January he tried a different tack, pleading for mercy towards those already detained, sending his wife Mary to intercede with Nottingham on his behalf, and making an extraordinarily pathetic confession:

My Lord a Body Unfit to bear the hardships of a Prison, and a Mind Impatient of Confinement, have been the Onely Reasons for withdrawing My Self; And My Lord the Cries of a Numerous Ruin'd Family, the Prospect of Long Banishment from my Native Country, and the hopes of her Majties Mercy, Moves me to Thro' my self at her Majties Feet, and to Entreat your Lordships Intercession.

Then, in another quite bizarre misreading of the circumstances in which he found himself, Daniel Defoe volunteers to serve as a cavalry officer, 'a year or More', for the Queen in the Netherlands, raising a troop at his own expense, 'and without Doubt my Lord I shall Dye There Much More To her Service than in a Prison'.[48] Evidently, he continued to believe that he could plea-bargain. With no author upon whom to lay the hands of the law, Nottingham ordered the Public Hangman to burn the text in New Palace Yard in February. Two months later, still thinking that his offer to serve in the cavalry might work, but recognising that a different route was essential, Defoe turned to his friend William Paterson with the request to seek Harley's understanding of his predicament. However, Paterson's letter did not reach the Speaker until 28 May, by which time Defoe had been betrayed and captured in the house of one Sammen, a French weaver living in Spitalfields.

The prisoner was taken immediately to Newgate Prison, the twelfth-century gaol on the site of the present Old Bailey, which Defoe would describe in lurid detail in *Moll Flanders*. Upon payment he was held in Press Yard, away from the most insanitary dungeons but still in the company of a murderer, a 'french spy', and a felon on an unspecified charge. Dismal Nottingham interrogated him fiercely on a number of occasions, apparently convinced that Defoe formed part of a wider conspiracy. He continued to deny this, and must have been sufficiently plausible that he was released on bail of £1,500, of which he personally paid a third, on 5 June. His trial a month later was presided over by six judges, almost every one of which had been offended either directly or indirectly by the accused's polemics over Occasional Conformity or manners, the recorder Salathiel Lovell being described by Defoe as having 'Neither Manners, nor Wit'. But it didn't really matter since he followed the advice of his counsel, one of the Kentish petitioners, to plead guilty. Even by the severe standards of the day the sentence was unduly harsh: to stand in the pillory three times, to pay a fine of two hundred marks (some £135), and to remain in Newgate until he could obtain 'good sureties to be of good behaviour for the space of seven years'. In short, Defoe was to be physically punished—the pillory was a dangerous place to be for anybody, let alone a controversialist with many enemies—fined, and, most importantly, closed down as a writer.[49]

The punishment was put on hold for the better part of a month as Defoe's friend William Penn petitioned for merciful reconsideration—pilloried men lost their right to vote and sit on juries—and the Queen called a Privy Council at Windsor, where, on 21 July she, together with Nottingham and the Earl of Godolphin, the Lord High Treasurer, heard Defoe explain in person why he had written *The Shortest Way*. She was not impressed; on 27 July Nottingham wrote to the sheriff, 'Her Majesty does not think fit to delay any longer the execution of the Sentence upon Mr Fooe' on 29, 30, and 31 July. It looked bad; the rains were abnormally heavy that month, which, even though it was summer, would in itself pose a threat to the health of a person held tight in the stocks for a number of hours. At the same time, to enhance the disgrace associated with the pillory, Defoe was held on the first occasion in Cornhill, within yards of his family home. A man of over forty with seven children and a professional reputation seemed set for ignominy. But Daniel Defoe transformed the occasion into a triumph. According to legend, it was fresh flowers, not eggs and tomatoes, that were thrown in symbolic repudiation of the law.

What did he do, this man who had admitted to cowardice and pleaded for mercy on the grounds of his personal vulnerability? He wrote a defiant poem, even before he entered the stocks, breaking within days the sentence of seven years' dutiful compliance. Defoe probably drafted *A Hymn to the*

Pillory immediately after his sentence—at 430 lines it was much shorter than *The True-Born Englishman* but still not short—and with the clear plan that it should be sold to onlookers as he stood in the '*State-Trap* of the Law', saluted with resolve from the opening lines:

> Hail *Hi'roglyphick* State Machin,
> Contriv'd to Punish Fancy in:
> Men that are Men, in thee can feel no Pain
> And all thy *Insignificants* disdain.

Defoe then runs through a history of previous distinguished victims of state corporal punishment before moving with almost insolent dispatch right back to the very subject of *The Shortest Way,* for which he was currently being punished:

> There would the Fam'd S[achevere]ll stand,
> With Trumpet of Sedition in his Hand,
> Sounding the first *Crusado* in the Land.
> He from a Church of *England* Pulpit first
> All his Dissenting Brethren Curst;
> Doom'd them to Satan for a Prey,
> And first found out *the shortest way*;
> With him the Wise Vice-Chancellor o'th' Press . . .

Following this attack on Oxford for licensing Sacheverell's sermon and a review of conflicts developing in the wider world, Defoe reverts to a

The bust of Daniel Defoe at the Hackney Museum. Photo by Sarah Ainslie.

denunciatory discourse worthy of the *Legion's Memorial* and far, far more dangerous:[50]

> They that in vast Employments rob the State, still bears the Bell.
> See them in *thy Embraces* meet their Fate;
> Let not the Millions they by Fraud obtain,
> Protect 'em from the Scandal, or the Pain:
> They who from Mean Beginnings grow
> To vast Estates, but God knows how;
> Who carry untold Sums away,
> From little Places, with but little Pay:
> Who costly Palaces Erect,
> The Thieves that built them to Protect . . .

The non-juror and Jacobite Charles Leslie, aghast at such bold provocation, protested at the 'Party' surrounding the prisoner, not just to protect him, but to sell his writings:

> And the Party causing his Books to be Hauk'd and Publickly Sold about the pillory, while he stood upon it (in Triumph!) for Writing them. And Writes on still. And the Advertisements in our News papers are fill'd with New Editions of his Works, among which this Shortest way, for which he was Pillory'd still bears the Bell.[51]

Perhaps Defoe had nothing more to lose when embarking on this course? He could not expect any early release. His Tilbury factory was collapsing even as he was imprisoned, debts building up again, and his family had to move in with his in-laws. Maybe he felt like the man who he described in *An Essay Upon Projects,* 'to be Absolutely without Three things, *Money, Friends,* and *Health,* he Dies in a Ditch, or in some worse place, a hospital'.[52]

In fact, Daniel Defoe had friends aplenty, as well as a supportive brother-in-law Robert Davis, a Tilbury shipwright, who had by early November stumped up enough money to cover a bond for keeping the peace. Further entreaties on his behalf were being written. But this was not enough. Maybe Defoe's defiance had cost him extra months of incarceration, and maybe Godolphin, Nottingham, and Harley had deliberately hung him out to dry in desperation—on 20 September Speaker Harley wrote to Godolphin, 'Foe is much oppressed in his mind'—but just as there was a price for virtue, so was there a reward for error. Daniel Defoe had shown himself such an agile wordsmith that the very government against which he had inveighed could now make good use of his services. On 4 November 1703 Godolphin authorised a secret service payment of £150 to cover Defoe's outstanding fine and Newgate fees.[53]

He was out. On 14 January he was formally discharged. On 31 July Queen Anne granted him the second royal pardon of his life. Defoe had absolutely no formal contract, but he had become a hired scribe and agent of the state. For the next nine years he would single-handedly and anonymously write and edit the *Review,* appearing two then three times a week, in the interest of the government of the day. All the while he corresponded with Harley and Godolphin secretly on matters of intelligence. It was a perfect combination—he could write noisily in safety and spy silently at the same time.

The Public Sphere

At first glance it might seem strange that the German radical theorist Jurgen Habermas, writing in the early 1960s, might make reference to Robert Harley, who, when he took up Daniel Defoe as a hired hack, was effectively leading the government and on his way to becoming the Earl of Oxford. In *Strukturwandel der Offlichkeit*, published in German in 1962 but not in English until 1989 (as *The Structural Transformation of the Public Sphere*), Habermas makes the case that the cultures of social control and the distinction between 'public' and 'private' had changed over time, corresponding in broad terms to classical, feudal, and bourgeois epochs in Germany, France, and Britain before collapsing during the twentieth century in the face of a consumerist onslaught as well as political conflict.

> By the 'public sphere' we mean first of all a realm of our social life in which something approaching public opinion can be formed. Access is granted to all citizens. A portion of the public sphere comes into being in every conversation in which private individuals assemble to form a public body. They then behave neither like business or professional people transacting private affairs, not like members of a constitutional order subject to the legal constraints of a state bureaucracy.[54]

Habermas saw the institutional shifts towards such a civil society as emerging from the 1690s in Britain, identifying as illustrative landmarks the Licensing Act of 1695, which abolished censorship and which Queen Anne could not persuade Parliament to repeal, and the Stamp Tax of 1712, which subjected the press to fiscal control, but succeeded only in reducing print-runs and titles, not overall liberties. (Between 1695 and 1714, despite the introduction of fifteen parliamentary bills, it proved impossible to institute prior censorship of printed matter.) Having limited access to a still underdeveloped historiography, Habermas did not mention the Copyright Act of 1710, which effectively took authorship into a full contractual embrace or—and this certainly needs mentioning—the Riot Act of 1715, required because none of these reforms of the printing and publishing regime could sensibly be expected to deliver in the real world the kind of narcotic conversation of which German philosophy sometimes stands accused. None the less, it is worth recalling the sentiments at the heart of *Legion's Memorial* and Habermas's reference to the discussion of 'representation' by Hans-Georg Gadamer:

> The history of this word is very informative. The Romans used it, but in the light of the Christian idea of the incarnation and the mystical body it acquired a completely new meaning. Representation now no longer means 'copy' or 'representation in a picture' . . . but 'replacement' . . . *Repraesentare* means 'to make present' . . . The important thing about the legal idea of representation is that the *persona repraesentata* is only the person represented, and yet the

representative, who is exercising the former's right, is dependent on him.[55]

Habermas picked up early on Ian Watt's longstanding interest in readerships and audiences. He did not have the sources to know that in 1714, 45 per cent of men and 25 per cent of women in England could at least read, and the levels were almost certainly higher in Scotland.[56] Academies like that at Newington Green would disappear under the Schism Act of 1714, but in a sense this loss—not condemned at all by Defoe—reflected the passage of history rather than a new politico-religious offensive; there were at least five hundred grammar schools in the country although it would take another hundred fifty years before Defoe's plans for a university in London would come to fruition.

For Habermas,

> Harley was the first statesman to understand how to turn the new situation to his advantage. He engaged authors like Defoe (who has been called the first professional journalist), who defended the cause of the Whigs not only in the pamphlets in use until then but also in the new journals. Indeed, he was first to make the 'party spirit' a 'public spirit'. Defoe's *Review*, Tutchin's *Observator*, and Swift's *Examiner* were discussed in clubs and coffeehouses, at home and in the streets.[57]

Aside from Watt, in terms of English sources Habermas relied on the work of Maurice Dobb and Raymond Williams, which may explain why he effectively promoted Defoe over Tutchin and Swift in this passage. However, he did also make reference to *The Spectator* of Addison and Steele (who interviewed Alexander Selkirk), which sold some 2,000 copies weekly between 1711 and 1714, and, along with Swift's short-lived paper in the Tory interregnum after 1710, was more widely distributed than the *Review*, registered at some 425 copies but issued thrice a week. It is, then, quite easy to over-emphasise the physical range of this new 'sphere'. However, as Craig Calhoun has noted, it is useful to think beyond the physical places noted by Habermas here, considering also the 'imagined community' along the lines suggested by Benedict Anderson for print capitalism enhancing a popular sense of nationhood in the nineteenth-century western hemisphere.[58]

For Markman Ellis, 'The distinctive features of coffee-house sociability were egalitarianism, congeniality, and conversation', and there is quite enough circumstantial evidence that Defoe used houses as more than post offices.[59] However, the Habermas thesis has been subjected to a number of criticisms over its omissions and exclusions. For the eighteenth century these are perhaps most telling in terms of religion, which, as we have seen, was still bitterly divisive, and the plebeian majority, which may well have lived in the city but were decidedly not 'bourgeois'. For a later period the principal critique has concerned the absence of women from the picture— serious issues which Habermas recognised long after what was effectively a Ph.D. thesis had been published.

Historians can be quite sniffy about model-building social scientists who don't themselves conduct research in the archives. But J.A. Downie's belief that Habermas 'misunderstands the nature of English society . . .

[and] offers an unreconstructed Marxist interpretation of English history according to which a bourgeois revolution had to have taken place by 1700' is a pretty severe judgement. Moreover, it does itself underestimate both the 'spirit of party' prevailing in Defoe's day and the extent to which 'the public was a fiction that was constructed through literary as well as political means'.[60] Mark Knights, who is much more sympathetic to the Habermas thesis, notes that 'the public' is first defined as a collective noun, rather than an adjective, in a dictionary of 1696—right in the midst of what we might call the 'swing decade'.[61] Yet Raymond Williams, whose work did so much to encourage intellectual engagement with 'the public', did not himself include it in his *Keywords*.

Rather than unreconstructed Marxism, Habermas seemed to have hit on a vital vector of a transitional social formation where, in E.P. Thompson's view,

> political power . . . may best be understood, not as a direct organ of any class or interest, but as a secondary political formation, a purchasing-point from which other kinds of economic and social power were gained or enhanced . . . for at least the first seven decades of the century we can find no industrial or professional middle class which exercises an effective curb upon the operations of predatory oligarchic power . . .

However, Thompson notes some important exceptions to the image of pure parasitism: the independent lesser gentry; the press, 'itself a kind of middle-class presence, in advance of other articulated expression'; the law, 'elevated during this century to a role more prominent than at any other period of our history'; and, finally, 'the ever-present resistance of the crowd'.[62] Perhaps, if he had been more interested in institutional politics, he might have added that the combination of all these elements was nowhere more evident than in the holding of elections, where, from 1695 to 1714, more men could vote, as a proportion of the adult male population, than at any other time before the 1867 Reform Act. In sum, even in his new role Daniel Defoe found himself at the centre, not of attention but of influence.

*

Defoe was released from Newgate in the first week of November 1703, being thrust right into the eye of the storm of Friday, 26 November 1703, which lasted for some seven hours into Saturday morning. This unusually violent cyclone killed upwards of eight thousand people—many, we have seen, at sea—and caused very extensive damage in London as well as the south and midlands of England and Wales. Defoe duly noted in *The Storm* (1704), his first full-length book, that as a consequence of the destruction the price of tiles rose 'from 21s. *per* Thousand to 6l. for plain Tiles; and from 50s. *per* Thousand for Pantiles, to 10l. and Bricklayers Labour to 5s. per Day'.[63] If he had been able to hold on to his Tilbury business he would assuredly have made a fortune.

But now as a journalist he set about his new trade in an innovative and engaging manner by advertising in the *Daily Courant* (2 December) and the very paper that had earlier carried the warrant for his arrest, the *London*

Gazette (2–6 December), requesting eyewitness accounts of the experience of the tempest:

> To preserve the Remembrance of the late Dreadful Tempest, an exact and faithful Collection is preparing of the most remarkable Disasters which happened on that Occasion, with the Places where, and Persons concern'd, whether at Sea or on Shore . . . All Gentlemen that are pleas'd to send any such Accounts, are desired to write no Particulars but that they are well satisfied to be true, and to set their Names to the Observations they send, which the Undertakers of this Work promise shall be faithfully Recorded, and the Favour publickly acknowledged.[64]

Plenty of letters were sent in, many by clergymen, whose contributions Defoe sometimes reproduced at length, surely believing, as he wrote in the Preface, 'Preaching of Sermons is Speaking to a few of Mankind: Printing of Books is Talking to the Whole World'.[65] Here also we find something of a reflective preamble to *Crusoe*:

> The main Inference I shall pretend to make or at least venture the exposing to publick View, in this case, is, the strong Evidence God has been pleas'd to give in this terrible manner to his own Being, which Mankind began more than ever to affront and despise . . . I cannot believe any Man so rooted in Atheistical Opinions, as not to find some Cause to doubt whether he was not in the Wrong, and a little to apprehend the Possibility of a Supreme Being, when

he felt the terrible Blasts of this Tempest. I cannot doubt but the Atheist's harden'd Soul trembl'd a little as well as his House . . .[66]

It is perhaps unsurprising that after 180 pages of descriptions and reflections on the hurricane, Defoe issued a brief *Lay-Man's Sermon on the late Storm*, and the first passages of the main book studiously 'allow the High Original of Nature to be the Great Author of all her Actings, and by the strict Rein of his Providence, is the Continual and Exact Guide of her Executive Power'.[67] This not only squared with Locke's 'Reasonableness of Christianity' but also provided a kind of dress rehearsal for key passages of a book still fifteen years in the future.

The wind was the issue naturally at the heart of this fiercely executive nature:

. . . the Winds are some of those Inscrutables of Nature, in which humane Search has not yet been able to arrive at any Demonstration . . . 'The Winds', *says the Learned Mr* Bohun, 'are generated in the Intermediate Space between the Earth and the Clouds, either by Rarefaction or Repletion, and sometimes haply by pressure of Clouds, Elastical Virtue of the Air, etc., from the Earth or Seas, as by Submarine or Subterranean Eruption or Descension or Resilition from the middle Region.[68]

There is a clear link between passages such as these and the science fiction of *The Consolidator*, published the following year as an allegory about a journey to the moon in which the 'Crolians' represented the Dissenters and form their own bank to help the boycott of their 'Solunarian' enemies. The images in the story are extraordinarily innovative, involving communication between China and the moon, where there exists a species of lunar telepathy, a truth-revealing telescope, 'elevators' that enabled communion with departed souls, and a lie-detecting chair. Perhaps these contrivances were too much for his readership, and the work, which is definitely strained in expression, attracted little popular attention, but it also failed to get Defoe into trouble with the very authorities for which he was now working.

Much more successful, and just as odd, was a ghost story of the same year, *A True Relation of the Apparition of One Mrs Veal, the next Day after her Death: to One Mrs. Bargrave at Canterbury the Eighth of September 1705*. This had apparently been attached to the sheets of a slow-selling moral text, Drelincourt's *The Christian's Defence against the Fears of Death* in order to spice it up. However, as a good Protestant, Defoe was here definitely allowing artistic licence to trump doctrinal conviction since, for all his considerable attraction to the supernatural as well as the natural, he believed that the dead went directly either to heaven or hell, with no intermediate dalliance in Purgatory allowable.

All this time Defoe was travelling throughout the country to collect political intelligence, so maybe he had more time to read and write than at home, or maybe his imagination was accelerated by the move of that home to Hackney in 1705. In any event, during these years Daniel Defoe appears to be engaged in a campaign to display his qualities as a polymath, and in 1706 he published *Jure Divino*, which he had started in Newgate and which is these days mostly notable for the Van de Gucht portrait from the frontispiece (and now in the National Portrait Gallery) although Defoe described it as a copy of a copy and 'about as much like the Author, as Sir *Roger l'Estrange*, was like the Dog *Towzer*'.[69] *Jure Divino* is even longer a poem than *The True-Born Englishman*, and much less original as a work either of creative writing or of political argumentation, being against the divine right of kings, against the doctrine of passive obedience, and against absolutism. Defoe thought that it would cause much more trouble than it did, perhaps because the work proceeds directly from the premise that 'All Men *would be Tyrants* if they cou'd' to *'all Kings would tyrannize'*. However, he had plainly learned the lessons of *The Shortest Way*, and ended the poem not only with a panegyric on Queen Anne but also a celebration of constitutional government.

Paula Backscheider suggests that *Jure Divino*, whilst it may have been composed in the style of Dryden and Rochester (strictly without the bawdiness), is the work that most closely links Defoe to John Locke:

Putting their trust in man's long-suffering nature, Locke and Defoe denied anarchy, chaos, or near continual unrest to be the consequences of their position. Both saw resistance as inevitable: 'how they will be hindered . . . I cannot tell', Locke wrote, and Defoe gave nearly two full books of his poem to historical example of nations finally driven to resistance after years of persecution and suffering.[70]

Perhaps Defoe felt constitutionally drawn to the ethos of resistance because of his own adverse experience in the world of business and debt, which he described in the *Review* of July 1705 in a candid, personal manner. This strongly suggests that he was not simply churning out propaganda for Harley (although he wrote to him in August 1706 in thankful celebration of the bankruptcy reform act), that Thompson was right about the importance of the law, and that financial skulduggery abounded:

> Sham actions, arrests, sleeping debates in trade of 17 years' standing revived; debts put in suits after contracts and agreements under hand and seal; and which is worse, writs taken out for debts without the knowledge of the creditor, and some after the creditor has been paid; diligent solicitations of persons not inclined to sue, pressing them to give him trouble; others offering to buy assignations of debts that they might be sued; for others to turn setters and informers to betray him into the hands of trouble; collateral bonds where the securities have been resigned and accepted . . .[71]

Yet just a month later, Defoe wrote to Harley from Tiverton, Devon, to inform that his correspondence had got him into a spot of bother of an only partly financial nature:

> The Misscarriage at Weymo[uth] happened by Such a Cassualty as no Man could foresee; my Letters, Directed for the Friend Now with me Call'd Capt Turner, to be left at Weymo[uth], were Taken up, by one Capt Turner, Commander of a Guernsey privateer Then in that Port. The Ignorant Tarr when he found things written Darke and Unintelligible shows them to all the

Town. At our Comeing however he Restores the Letters, Drank a pint of wine with us and Calls for One himself, which it seems afterward he went away, and Never paid for. The people of the house Demanding Money for it next Day Put him a frett, and that Vented it Self in his Railing at this Letter all about Town Till the Mayor sent for him. The Imperfect account he gave fills the Mayors as foolish head with Jealousyes, and the Assizes being at Dorchester, away he Runs to the Judges and Getts a Summons . . .

Defoe was not undercover in person—only his activities were—so out went the warrant, which would not contain the last mention of 'false news' in Anglo-Saxon political history:

To all Constables and Tythingmen and other her majesties officers within the County of Devon and also to Charles Sugg.

Whereas I have received Information against Daniel de Foe for spreading and publishing divers seditious and scandalous Libels and false news to the great disturbance of the Peace of this Kingdom and that He is a person of ill Fame and Behaviour, and is now lurking within some or one of your Parishes, Tythings, or Precincts . . .

Defoe was able to slip away unarrested to Cornwall, but made sure that he sent another letter—to the magistrate who ordered his detention:

I do my Selfe the Honour to acquaint you that foreseeing the possibility of Such dealings I have with me a Certification from her matyes Secretary of State of my having acquainted the Government of my Occasions to travele and of my giving Security for my Fidelity . . . By this Sir I publickly Confute, that Scandalous Falsity affirmed in your warrant of my Lurking in the Countrey, and I am Sorry my Occasions will not permit to tell you soe to your face.

And for Harley, who had an appetite for secrecy and conspiracy every bit as acute as his own, Defoe offered reassurance:

As to Apprehensions of my Friend who is with me betrayeing me, I assure you to the Contrary, Nor are you Sir betraid to him, Nor does he suspect I Correspond with you or have the honour to Converse with you. I am not Serving a Master I have so little Vallue for. You may Sir Depend upon me That Neither by Fraud or Folly the Confidence you are pleasd to place in me shall ever be Dissappointed.[72]

Harley was convinced, and sufficiently so that the following summer he sent Defoe to Edinburgh, to report on the local response to the negotiations over the union of England and Scotland that appeared to be coming to a head.

Spying on the Squadrone

It isn't clear if Defoe had visited Scotland before arriving there at Harley's behest in September 1706 after a long, wet, and uncomfortable journey.

This would be the first of three protracted stays over the following four years and a short visit in 1712. Defoe's presence was required not just to monitor and influence the initial response to the negotiations of union, but also to report on elite and popular reaction to the agreement of May 1707, not least because its contentious terms opened up local and international conflict, with an abortive French invasion in 1708 and the Jacobite rising of 1715.

Before he left Defoe had already picked up on the need to address negative English dismissiveness and apprehension about the threat to the Episcopalian Church of England by Scottish Presbyterianism, addressing this in the *Review* once he returned from his tour of the English West Country. Scottish Presbyterianism was quite distinct from that in England in that it was effectively the established national Church, not a dissenting minority based on individual congregations, and had a system of governance under the Kirk, which was a major political player both at elite and popular levels. Writing in December 1705, with only his Scottish contacts in London as reliable sources—and much of Defoe's writing on Scotland was interested, partial, and unreliable—he sought to reassure his English readers that the Scots would always be,

Unanimous, Hearty, Zealous and Faithful, both in Matters of Religion, and all Civil Interests; they will go hand in hand with you in every thing that's reasonable to the settling Religion and *English liberty*.[73]

Such reassurance was necessary as a result of nationalist feelings heightened by the issue of dynastic succession, always likely to be a flashpoint since the union of the crowns from 1603 in the person of James VI/I and carried forward for almost a century through male and female members of the Stuart family although only James I and Charles I had been born in Scotland (Edinburgh and Dunfermline respectively). As a result, when Queen Anne's last surviving child, the Duke of Gloucester, died in 1700, the English Parliament passed the Act of Settlement to ensure the Hanoverian succession without any consultation with its Scots counterpart, where 157 MPs might be thought to have a vested interest in such a matter. Accordingly, the Edinburgh parliament passed an Act of Security in 1704, reserving the right of Scotland to choose a successor to Anne independently of the English and their legislation. In a rather predictable process of tit-for-tat, reminiscent of modern trade wars, Westminster duly responded with the Aliens Act of 1705, declaring that until such time as the Scots Security Act was repealed the Scots would be regarded as aliens in England, stopping at a stroke Scottish exports of livestock, coal, and linen.[74]

If we compare this standoff with the eventual terms of the union two years later we can gain a sense of the balance of power and the wider circumstances in which Defoe was working openly as an agent of influence and clandestinely as an informer. First, a single kingdom of 'Great Britain' was formed of England, Scotland, and Wales (which had been in union with England since 1536 and, although 80 per cent of its people spoke Welsh, was small, geographically divided and not a politico-military threat). Secondly, the Hanoverian succession was agreed, and a single Parliament established at Westminster to include, as a distinct minority, forty-five MPs from Scottish constituencies and sixteen elected Scottish peers. In the new British free trade area, English standards of coin, weights, and measures would prevail (Scottish pounds and pence were worth about a twelfth of their English counterparts; Scottish pints and gallons were three times those of the English). The English fiscal system would now apply to all of Great Britain, but there would be equality of status in colonial trade. No change would be made to Scotland's legal system, burghs, heritable jurisdictions, universities, or the Presbyterian Settlement. This last feature effectively resolved the potential threat deriving from the National Covenant of 1638 and the Solemn League and Covenant of 1643 of the Civil War era by which doctrinal convergence was predicated and which, of course, had been challenged by the 1662 Act of Uniformity. Now the Church of England did not seek to impose a minority Episcopalian order whilst the Kirk compromised by recognising ministers who had been ordained by bishops.[75] If this seems abstruse in the twenty-first century, one need only think of the referendums of 2014 over Scottish independence and 2016 over Brexit to glean a sense of how religious markers of independence have been updated in nationalist and economic terms.

Moreover, there was in 1707 plenty of straight economic haggling. At the heart of this was Scottish participation in the new and fast expanding national debt. Here Westminster had to make substantial compensation—known as the 'Equivalent'—of £400,000, which also covered those who had invested in the disastrous enterprise to establish a Scottish colony in Panama (the 'Darien Scheme', which collapsed in 1700) and the losses incurred in adopting the hard English coinage of 1696. In addition, £20,000 was distributed to Scottish office holders to cover expenses and arrears that was recognised from the off as a substantial bribe selectively distributed. The English House of Commons agreed to these terms with minimal debate. In Scotland, by contrast, over five hundred pamphlets were published on the Union, and public opinion was bitterly divided, the Marquess of Tweedale's young and impressively named *Squadrone Volante* that Defoe later described in conclusive terms:

> The Hot Presbyterians called The Squadroni—These are by a kind of Principle allwayes against the Court, Right or wrong. They were so in King Williams Time, And were So in The Last Ministry, And Are so Still; And Are indeed worthy to be lay'd Aside by Every Party that purpose to keep the Government in bounds.[76]

If Daniel Defoe had no say whatsoever in the deliberations of the Commissioners in London, we know from his acknowledgement of instructions received some nine months before the Union, that the Scottish reaction had been fully anticipated by Harley:

1. To Inform My Self of the Measures Takeing Or Partys forming Against the Union and Applye my Self to prevent them.
2. In Conversation and by all reasonable Methods to Dispose peoples minds to the Union.

3. By writing or Discourse, to Answer any Objections, Libells or Reflections on the Union, the English or the Court, Relateing to the Union.

4. To Remove the Jealousies and Uneasyness of people about Secret designs here against the Kirk etc . . .[77]

In the same letter Defoe then raises a matter that recurs throughout his correspondence—usually signed either with a symbol or as 'Claude Guilot'—with Harley: the matter of payment. We now know from the secret service accounts that he received £850 between September 1710 and July 1714.[78] Moreover, he had received a very substantial gift from the Marlboroughs in 1705. But at the start of his Edinburgh operation, Defoe seems not to be exaggerating overly in his worries over cash flow. He had yet to set up northern commercial deals or publish the Edinburgh edition of the *Review* that would provide an income as well as support his mission between June 1708 and June 1710.

Harley, knowing Defoe's penchant for misguided candour almost matched his appetite for secrecy, went out of his way in urging caution on his agent:

1. You are to use the utmost caution that it may not be supposed you are employed by any person in England: but that you came there upon your own business, and out of love from the Country . . .

2. You may confidently assure those you converse with, that the Queen and all those who have Credit with her, are sincere and heart for the Union.

3. You must shew them, this is such an opportunity that being once lost or neglected is not again to be recovered. England never was before in so good a disposition to make such large Concessions, or so heartily to unite with Scotland, and should their kindness now be slighted . . .[79]

In fact, Defoe was sufficiently cowed by displays of anti-Union sentiment on the streets that he several times made mention in his letters to the fate of Jan de Witt, the Dutch statesman torn to pieces by a mob in 1672, and he deemed it judicious to curry favour in poetic form:

I am writeing a Poem in praise of Scotland. You will say that it is an odd subject, to bear a Panegyrick, but my End will be answerd. I make them believ I am Come away from England, and resolv if the Union goes on to settle in Scotland, and all Conduces to perswade them I am a friend to their Country . . .[80]

Just quite how successful that form of expression might prove to be was, however, put into a question by Defoe's dispatch of two weeks later:

At Dumfries They have burnt the Articles in the market place. At Glasgow They were about it but the Magistrates prevaild with them to forebear On promise to sign an address against it.

It would amaze you if I should give you the Trouble of Repeating The Ridiculous Notions people here have Entertaind Against Their Own happiness. The Libells, The Absurdities and The Insults on That head are Intollerable.

The High Commissioner has had Letters Sent to Threaten with Pistoll, Dagger and a Variety of Assassination, and the Unusuall Numbers of Highlanders Makes some People Very Uneasy here, There being More of Them here now than has been known— Indeed they are Formidable Fellows and I Onely Wish Her Majtie had 25000 of them in spain, a Nation Equally proud and Barbarous like Themselves.[81]

Defoe, none the less, wanted to reassure Harley that his mission was yielding results:

. . . you shall not be Uneasy at your Trusting me here. I have compass'd my First and Main step happily Enough, in That I am Perfectly Unsuspected as Corresponding with anybody in England. I converse with Presbyterian, Episcopall-Dissenter, papist and Non-Juror, and I hope with Equall Circumspection. I flatter my Self that you will have no Complaints of my Conduct. I have faithfull Emissaries in Every Company And I Talk to Everybody in Their Own way. To the Merchants I am about to Settle here in Trade, Building ships etc. With the Lawyers I Want to purchase a House and Land to bring my Family and Live upon it (God knows where the Money is to pay for it). To day I am Goeing

into Partnership with a Membr of parliament in a Glass house, to
morrow with Another in a Salt work. With the Glasgow Mutineers
I am to be a fish Merchant, with the Aberdeen Men a woollen and
with the Perth and western Men a Linen Manufacturer, and still
at the End of all Discourse the Union is the Essentiall and I am
all to Every one that I may Gain some.[82]

Such comprehensive fibbing—no doubt encouraged by the large quantities
of wine and spirits being imported into Scotland before the customs union
came into effect—seems to have swollen Defoe's head:

In my Mannagemt here I am a pefect Emissary. I act the Old
part of Cardinall Richlieu. I have my spyes and my pensioners
In Every place, and I Confess 'tis the Easyest thing in the World
to hire people here to betray their Friends . . . I have spies in the
Commission, in the parliament, and in the assembly, and Undr
pretence of writeing my history I have Every Thing told me.[83]

Yet by the time of the final agreement, it is Defoe who is urging Harley
to appoint as customs and excise officers only men capable of displaying
'Courtisye, Civillity and Calmness' for fear of provoking a violent backlash.
When, in August 1707 the convoy bringing the 'Equivalent' to Edinburgh
approached the castle it came under physical attack, not for the purposes of
robbery but as an expression of popular outrage at being bought off:

It is not to be Described the Fury and Indignation of the people.
On the Sight of it, Cursing Their Own Guards that brought it

in, stoneing the Poor Fellows That Drew the Waggons. Nay the Very Horses. I Saw One of the Waggon Drivers Wounded with a stone On the Face which if it had not Glanced On his shoulder First I believ had Certainly Killed him—They Call it the Price of their Country and the poor people Are Incens'd by the Subtill Jacobites and too much by some of the Presb. Ministers—that they go along the streets Curseing the Very English Nation.[84]

The popular ardour was not, however, matched by political and logistical planning by the Jacobite elite or Louis XIV so that the delayed and disorganised effort at invasion in March 1708 was an abject military failure. It does, though, seemed to have concentrated political minds, with the Whigs readily winning the election that June, so that Defoe was now working for Godolphin, who paid up much more readily than Harley but may have been too affable in assuring this man who lied so prodigiously for his country, 'I always think a man honest till I find to the contrary'.[85]

In fact, not all Defoe's stories were complete fabrications. He did trade in wines, and even promised Harley a cut-price barrel of claret. He provided advice to friends and informants on china, plate, and even pickles.[86] Moreover, his second son, Benjamin, attended Edinburgh University in 1710–11 before messing up his studies badly. Perhaps he was affected by the kind of political confusion reported by his father for the London edition of the *Review*:

. . . it is acknowledged that the outside is very mysterious. Both sides set up whigs, and both sides set up tories. They that would

214

be called the whig party vote for professed Jacobites; whigs set up tories against whigs; and Jacobites take the vote to qualify themselves to vote for whigs; and tories set up whigs against tories. In short, it is all a game of parties. The squadrons jostle in politics where they join in principle, and join in the means where they are opposites in the end.[87]

This was surely intended to amuse as much as illuminate his metropolitan readership, but it did signal that even with so few Scottish MPs in Westminster, British political life had acquired an even more complex character. Defoe's later visits to the country suggest that Harley saw the need to read the mood of Scotland in the wake of the Union, especially whilst the country remained at war with France. And it was to Harley that Defoe found himself reporting once more, as a result of the general election of October–November 1710 in which the Tories increased their presence in the Commons by over one hundred seats almost all at the expense of the Whigs, who had been dreading the poll. The reason was not the new Union, nor the course of the war, even though Marlborough's most recent victory at Malplaquet had been extremely costly in terms of casualties. The reason was the extraordinary fall-out from a sermon. And that sermon had been preached by Defoe's nemesis, the 'Bloody Flag Officer', Henry Sacheverell.

*

In 1708 Daniel Defoe looked to be in a comfortable position. Although some debts lingered, the gift from the Marlboroughs, the payments from the secret service account, and continued success of the *Review* all enabled him to move the family to a large house in Stoke Newington, acquire a carriage and a full complement of servants, and enjoy what leisure time he allowed himself reading in his capacious garden. Although he admitted that he disliked serving both Tory and Whig administrations, not least for the charges of opportunism it provoked, Defoe now deployed Godolphin's argument,

> That I was the Queen's Servant . . . My Business was to wait, and then apply my self to the Ministers of State, to receive her Majesty's Commands from them . . . [my] Duty . . . to go along with every Ministry, so far as they did not break in upon the Constitution, and the Laws and Liberties of my Country; my Part being only the Duty of a Subject, *(viz)* to submit to all lawful Commands.[88]

It was surely such changes in circumstances and convictions that made Defoe's reaction to Sacheverell's sermon of 5 November 1709 quite different to that of May 1702, which had provoked him into penning *The Shortest Way*. In fact, Defoe was in Scotland when Sacheverell preached at St. Paul's and so he didn't respond for a month. But that scarcely mattered given the scandal caused by the priest's response to the invitation by the Lord Mayor, Sir Samuel Garrard, to preach on a key day in the country's political calendar. Yet in 'On the Perils of False Brethren Both in Church and State', Sacheverell made no mention of the Gunpowder Plot or the landing of King William at Torbay in 1688. Moreover, he nowhere identified the Jacobites as 'false brethren', reserving that tag for the Dissenters. Most importantly, he emphatically denied that resistance to the King was ever lawful:

> These FALSE BRETHREN in *our Government*, do not *Singly*, and in *Private* spread their *Poyson*, but (what is lamentable to be spoken) are suffer'd to combine into *Bodies*, and *Seminaries*, wherein *Atheism, Deism, Tritheism, Socinianism*, with all the *Hellish Principles of Fanaticism, Regicide, and Anarchy*, are openly *Profess'd*, and *Taught*, to *Corrupt* and *Debauch* the *Youth* of the *Nation*, in all *Parts* of it, down to *Posterity*, to the *Present Reproach*, and *Future Extirpation* of Our *Laws* and *Religion*.

This tirade outdid anything Defoe had invented in 1702. The cleric clearly believed that he had *carte blanche* from the Lord Mayor to use the new cathedral as a platform for his righteous invective. But, as W.A. Speck, notes,

> It was his denial that there had been resistance in the Revolution which led to Sacheverell's impeachment. Such a blatant attack on the Whig view of 1688 could not be ignored by a party which had a majority in both houses of parliament.[89]

Accordingly, Sacheverell was duly summoned to be tried before Parliament. Defoe, surely mindful that the boot was now on the other foot, first urged his readers not to over-react:

> You should use him as we do a hot horse—when he first frets and pulls, keep a stiff rein, and hold him in if you can; but if he grows

mad and furious, slack your hand, clap your heels to him, and let him go, give him his belly full of it. Away goes the beast like a fury, over hedge and ditch, till he runs himself off of his mettle, perhaps hogs himself, and then he grows quiet of course.[90]

But he couldn't hold back for long, enjoying the opportunity to rail against the High Church with the implicit imprimatur of the ministry:

They expose their Designs, *viz.* To embroil this Nation in the old Broils about Conscience, Liberty, Tyranny, and Oppression of Property, Things all happily settled by the Revolution, effectually confirm'd by the Succession, and for ever secur'd by the Union— And, as it is apparent, these are their Grievances, let them grin, and snarl, and rail, the Mountain stands sure, the Glorious Pillar is rais'd, Revolution is the Basis, Protestant Succession is the Column, and Union is the Capital, Liberty, Religion, Peace and Truth are the beautiful Carv'd Work round it; and the QUEEN supported by Justice on one hand and Strength on the other, is its Guard and Defence.[91]

This must have been very gratifying to write, and it is almost as if Defoe was constructing in words what Wren and Hawksmoor had done with stone. But he did not return to London until late January 1710, and had badly misjudged the mood of the town. As Sacheverell's trial proceeded, Defoe started to note the level of popular support for the accused—'more like an Ambassador of State than a criminal going to the bar of justice'— and the shifting of attention from a supposed civil infraction to matters of religious piety. Three days after the trial opened, on the night of 1 March, a large crowd comprised largely of apprentices looted and burnt a number of Meeting Houses of Dissenters, shouting insults against the Bank of England, and requiring the deployment of the Horse Guards to restore order. No private buildings were assaulted, and nobody was killed, but the sentiment on the street reflected a strong Tory backlash.[92] Godolphin, who had led the case against Sacheverell, eventually secured a 69–52 vote for his guilt in the House of Lords, but only a six-vote majority for the prohibition from preaching for three years. Sacheverell was widely feted and made a triumphant progress to his new parish in Shropshire, tarrying conspicuously in Tory Oxford:

> The Dissenters and their Friends have foolishly Endeavour'd to raise a Disturbance throughout the whole Kingdon by Trying in most Great Towns, on the Coronation Day to Burn me in Effigie, to Inodiate my Person and Cause with the Populace: But if this Silly Strategem has produc'd a quite Contrary Effect, and turn's upon the First Authors, and aggressors, and the People have Express'd their Resentment in any Culpable way, I hope it is not to be laid to my Charge . . .[93]

Godolphin left office in August and died two years later. Sacheverell's name was chanted in riots against the coronation of George I in 1714, but the man himself played no prominent role in national politics thereafter. Defoe's ideology had been energetically expressed, but by the end of the year he would be writing for a rather different cause. Meanwhile, off the coast of Chile Woodes Rogers had just rescued Alexander Selkirk.

Learning the Hard Way

At the age of fifty, Defoe might have been expected to settle for a quiet life, but we already know him well enough to dismiss that option. He had a great deal more writing in him, and so, of course, the opportunities for misjudgement and mischief and the occasion of sheer bad luck, notwithstanding his formidable record in denial, shape-shifting, and voice throwing. At a time of international conflict, with the monarchical successions in Great Britain and Spain both under challenge and designated to foreigners, and the religious fissures of British society still raw, Defoe had to address plenty of contentious issues. Yet, in the wake of the Sacheverell riots, and in the face of growing disillusionment with an eight-year war that had been entered into as an alliance but conducted as a principal power, the political editor in him reverted to the *via media* as well as the main chance. In July 1710, before the general election, he wrote to Harley,

> I can Not but Think that Now is The Time to find Out and Improve Those blessed Mediums of this Nations happiness, which lye between The wild Extremes of all Partyes . . . . I can Not but hope that Heaven has yet Reserv'd you to be the Restorer of your Country by yet bringing Exasperated Parties and the Respective Mad-Men to Their Politick Sences . . . If I can be

Usefull to So Good a work without the Least View of Private
Advantage I should be Very Glad . . .[94]

It is unclear whether Defoe knew that Harley was readying to hire Swift
for this purpose, but he soon did take that course, so that the two personal competitors were writing for the same ministry, albeit from different
angles, which must have pleased the new Lord High Treasurer and recently
ennobled Earl of Oxford. Swift, who plainly had greater access, led the
propagandistic charge for the Tory mission to end the war by attacking
Marlborough, whose wife had been dismissed by Queen Anne from her
longstanding role as favourite and counsellor: '. . . whether this War were
prudently begun or not, it is plain, that the true Spring or Motive of it, was
the aggrandizing of a particular Family, and in short, a War of the *General*
and the *Ministry*, and not of the *Prince* or *People*'.[95] Defoe now held a preference for a maritime conflict, which could protect existing British trade
in the West Indies and open up new commerce in the South Atlantic and
Pacific. He probably knew less of the secret negotiations with the French in
1711, and his position over the terms of any peace wavered away from the
Whig slogan of 'No Peace without Spain' that scuppered the first round of
talks. But he was very worried by Harley's extraordinary ruse to form the
South Sea Company, which in June 1711 effectively privatised £9 million of
the national debt. As Glyn Williams notes,

> At the time, it had all the appearance of a master-stroke by Harley
> . . . He had disposed of the immediate problem of the floating debt;
> had set up a company with a directorate he could pack with those

221

Tory merchants, financiers and politicians who were excluded from the Whig-dominated Bank of England and East India Company; and was sure of support from the Tory country gentry and mercantile community for his move away from the endless continental campaigns towards the more alluring prospect of war or trade, or both in Spanish America.[96]

The Spanish, as we have seen, excluded all foreigners—even their French allies—from their American empire ('the Indies'), but they only had three ships to patrol the Pacific coastline from Tierra del Fuego to California. They looked to be a perfect target for what was one of the most extravagant scams in financial history. Robert Harley and Henry St. John, the xenophobic Secretary of State who was leading negotiations with the French, had absolutely no material grounds—let alone any legal basis—upon which to make the fantasy grant to the Company:

> The sole trade and traffick into, unto, and from all the kingdoms, lands, countries, territories, islands, cities, towns, ports, havens, creeks, and places of America, on the east side thereof from the river of Aranoca, to the southernmost part of the Terra del Fuego; and on the west side thereof, from the said southernmost part of the said Terra del Fuego, through the South Seas, to the northernmost part of America, and into, unto, and from all countries, islands, and places within the same limits, which are reported to belong to the Crown of Spain, or which shall hereafter be found

out or discovered within the said limits, not exceeding three hundred leagues from the continent of America.[97]

In the face of this extraordinary paper act of international expropriation Daniel Defoe had enough firm information and common sense to hedge his bets, even at the risk of alienating the ministry:

> What are we to understand by the Trade to the South Seas? I say frankly, If we mean that we shall take possession of some Port or Place, Ports or Places, on the West side of America . . . and that from this, or these Places, we shall carry on a free Trade with the Spaniards of America, throughout the rest of their Plantations, that is, with Peru, Mexico etc., as the French do now: If, I say, this is understood by the South-Sea Trade, then I must say, I doubt the Success of it, and that we can never carry on such a Trade, make 40 Acts of Parliament, Erect 40 Companies, and take possession of 40 Ports in the South-Seas. [98]

If these were not the words of a supplicant hack, two weeks later Defoe privately sent Harley a copy of a draft memorandum of his own to William III proposing precisely British settlements on the coasts of both North and South America, with a particular focus on Chile,

> Perticularly Proper for an English Collony, Because by The Scituation And Other Properties it is More Adapted For Commerce, Planting and inhabiting . . . This Country, as being too Remote, The Spaniards as if They had been Sated and Glutted

with the Wealth of Peru, Never Entirely Conquer'd; by which Means tho' They did posess The Coast, yet the Natives Remain, and Are Very Numerous, Hateing the Spaniards, and willing to Reciev any Nation That are Likely to Deliver Them from The Slavery They are Undr to the Cruell and Tyrannic Temper of the said Spaniards.[99]

The original papers, Defoe writes to Harley, no longer exist because 'my Lord Nottinghams fury forced me to Burn Them' in 1703. Indeed, in November 1711 Nottingham, who was a High Tory but not a member of the ministry, was not yet out of the picture, dismally trading his support for Whig objections to the proposed peace deal for the passage of a bill banning Occasional Conformity that he had been seeking for over a decade. For Defoe the entwining of the South Sea Project with the intricacies of domestic politics was little short of a disaster, less because of Occasional Conformity, to which he remained opposed, but because no good could come of combining the debt and the opening of Spanish America, 'to cure them both with One Plaister, or as we say more vulgarly, Kill both these Birds with One Stone'.

Daniel Defoe was not now trading as much as he was writing, but he still prided himself on his commercial acumen, and he could see trouble coming from the start:

. . . a trade, which had it been offered to the Merchandizing Part of Mankind, who understood Trade, who were employ'd in Commerce, and accustom'd to Adventures, and not unhappily

Ropemaker Lane. Photo by Sarah Ainslie.

join'd in and tied down to a Rabble of casual Subscribers, neither inclin'd to, capable of, or in the least having a Genius to trade, it would no doubt have met with another kind of Reception than now it has.[100]

When the bubble finally burst in 1720, Defoe was writing, as a species of Whig mole, in the conservative *Mist's Journal* (probably with Mist's knowledge of the effort to tone down Tory intemperance). His message was very similar to *An Essay Upon Projects* of 1697, but the tone more careworn:

It is by some, and those of no small Experience, thought strange to see the World so very fond of encouraging Projectors; and if we consider, that the Generality of Men . . . was it not too plain that their Heads are strangely disordered, and they can dream of nothing but getting large Estates, and setting up fine Equipages. Hence it is, that every Adventurer fancies himself Fortune's Favourite; and therefore, is resolved by no Means to let it be out of her Power to make him at once a Rich Man . . .[101]

*

The peace eventually agreed at Utrecht in 1713 to end the War of Spanish Succession did not meet the Whig demands for the removal of the Bourbon interest in Spain. It also left France contained by not much more than the renunciation of Philip V of Spain to any claim on the French throne whilst Louis XIV accepted the Protestant succession in Great Britain. This was vital to Defoe, but still insufficient because while Dutch Protestantism was defended, its mercantile status was not addressed:

> As for *my Opinion* of the Peace . . . *I do not like it at all* . . . but . . . *do not dislike it* for the same Reasons that some do . . . nor *did I like the Peace* you were making before . . . I aim'd at another kind of peace . . . A Peace that should have parted this Bone of Contention among all the Contenders, and particularly should have allotted such an Interest, such a Strength, and such a Commerce to *Britain* and *Holland*, as should have made the Protestant Interest Superior to all *Europe*.[102]

Moreover, he was prescient in his apprehensions about a Jacobite Rising. However, later in *The Secret History of the White Staff* (1715), written after Anne's death, the fall of the Tory ministry, the flight of St. John to join the Old Pretender in France, and the jailing of Oxford in the Tower of London, Defoe took great pains to defend Oxford's conduct. He also traduced others, such as the new favourite Abigail Masham ('The Female Buz . . . the Heifers of the Court') and St. John, drawing particular vituperation from resurgent Whig forces, which, headed by Robert Walpole, would dominate the political scene for the coming period:

> He is capable of such Drudgery as any Wretch alive, and can with a quiet Conscience publish a *Satyr* and a *Panegyrick* on the same Person, as very often he writes and answers himself. In this he sometimes is oblig'd to be honest by Necessity, and to make

himself appear as great a *Knave* and a *Dunce* in one scription, as he pretended to be a *Politician* and an *Englishman* in another. This juggling would be of great service to the late *Managers*, if it could take off People from talking on their crimes . . .[103]

There is a strong sense that Defoe's other prominent publication of 1715, *An Appeal to Honour*, a self-defence which was openly attributed to his authorship, derived directly from the experience of outright denigration. Moreover, in April 1713 Defoe's creditors had contrived his arrest on the back of another poorly judged foray into parodying his opponents through irony, which he never managed to master and which had landed him back in jail for eleven uncomfortable days. His defence was precisely that he did not mean what he wrote in the three dangerously entitled pamphlets— *Reasons against the Succession of the House of Hanover*; *And What if the Pretender Should Come? Or Some Considerations of the Advantages and Real Consequences of the Pretender's Possessing the Crown of Great Britain:* and—tempting fate to the very limit—*An Answer to a Question that nobody thinks of, viz., What if the Queen Should Die?* Luckily for Defoe he was charged only with libel under Chief Justice Thomas Parker, who was a Whig, but he still needed government bail.

The next year, of course, the Queen did die, at the age of forty-nine, and the Hanoverian succession proceeded as ordained by Parliament over the fifty-odd people who had superior dynastic claims to George I. The failure of the Jacobite rising in late 1715, despite reaching as far south as Preston, further reassured Daniel Defoe that his worst fears had been averted. But he had now rubbed almost everybody the wrong way. The

Review had run out of steam in the midst of the peace negotiations; the Dissenters disliked his support for suppressing Occasional Conformity; the Whigs despised his slippery movements not just over foreign policy but also over Oxford, whom they charged with high treason; and he now had no real friends at Court.

Defoe had one last shot at playing the political field through rhetoric in the double-bluff of *The Secret History of the Secret History of the White Staff* where he suggests that both Whig and Tory have 'been bubbled to accept these Romances for a true Narration, and have taken the Fable for History, without enquiring into the Things whether they were imposed upon, *Yea* or *No* . . . ' Later he invents a scene in which a friend visits Defoe to see whether the original *Secret History* had been composed on Oxford's instruction:

> It seems he found the poor Man in a very Dangerous Condition, having had a Fit of an Apoplexy, and being very Weak, insomuch as his Life was despair'd of; but, mentioning the said Books to him, and that the Town charg'd him with being the Author of them, and that he had Written them by Direction of the said Lord *Oxford*, the Person answer'd, That they did him a great deal of Wrong . . .[104]

Defoe kept on producing journalism, but his inventiveness needed somewhere new to go. He was now moving towards the composition of an outright fable, and hopefully one that would not land him in hot water.

The Work of Wordplay

The move from *The Secret History of the Secret History* to *Robinson Crusoe* was not direct—apart from anything else, Woodes Rogers's *Cruising Voyage*, which recounted the story of Selkirk, did not appear until 1718. Moreover, in his search for a profitable literary enterprise Defoe had alighted on the genre of conduct books that he would continue to produce after he had ceased to write narrative fiction in 1724. The first and most successful of the didactic books—eight editions sold out in five years—was *The Family Instructor* (1715), in which the parent-child relationship takes centre-stage and evidently prefigures the 'prodigal passages' of *Crusoe*. The book is a real hybrid, combining regularly reported ethical and moral reflections with invented 'dialogues':

> Their eldest Daughter was about eighteen Years old, and her Mother, it seems, began with her first; the Mother found it a very difficult matter to deal with her: For when she came to tell her of laying by her foolish Romances and Novels, *of which she was mighty fond*; leaving off her Patches and Play-Books; refusing her going to the Park on the Sabbath-days, *and the like*, she flew out in a Passion, and told her Mother *in plain Words* she would not be hinder'd, she was past a Child, she would go to the Park, and to the Play, *and the like*, ay that she would.

Her Mother responds strongly to the stubbornness.

Upon this Repulse she flings up Stairs into her Chamber, where she sat crying, when *her elder Brother*, whom the Father, it seems, had not yet begun with, came to her, between which Couple begins the following Dialogue.

Brother: Sister! What in Tears! What's the matter now?

She cries on, but makes no Answer

Bro.: Dear Sister! Tell me your grievance, *I say tell me*, what is it that troubles you?

And pulls her by her Cloaths

Sis.: I won't; don't trouble me, *I won't tell you*, let me alone.

Sobs and cries still.

Bro.: Prethee, what is the matter, *Sister*? Why, you will spoil your Face, you won't be fit to go to the Park; *come*, I came to have you *go out*, we will all go to the Park.

Sis.: Ay, so you may if you can.

Bro.: If I can! What do you mean by that? I have order'd *Thomas* to get the Coach ready.

Sis.: It's no matter for that, I can assure you *he won't do it*.

Bro.: I'll Cane the Rascal if he don't, *and that presently too*; come do you wipe your Eyes, and don't pretend to go Abroad with a blubber'd Face . . .

And so on, for several pages.[105]

As John Richetti also notes about *Religious Courtship* (1722), published the same year as *Moll Flanders*, Defoe's conduct books are 'intensely narrativized or dramatized'.[106] This is less true of *Conjugal Lewdness* (1727), but even there Defoe makes recourse to dialogue in defending his title:

> If any Man is displeased at my calling this by the nature of Matrimonial Whoredom, let him find a better Name for it, if he can, and tell me, what I shall call it, that is suitable to the Thing itself. If it is not lewd and scandalous, nay, openly declared Lewdness, what else must it be? What else can it be? I remember the Excuse a certain antient Lady gave for such a Marriage, had more Craft in it, tho' perhaps more Truth too, considering it Allegorically, than most of the lame Extenuations I generally meet with.

> DEAR Madam, says a neighbouring Gentlewoman, her Relation, to her, I hear your Ladyship is resolved to marry; I cannot say I believed it, for indeed I did not.

> WHY, Cousin, *says the Lady*, for such she was, why should you not believe it?

> NAY, Madam, *says she*, because for your own sake. I would not have it be true.

> WHY, Cousin, *says the Lady*, why would you not have it be true?

O, Madam, *says the Cousin*, you live so purely, to be so easy, so happy, so free, as you are, methinks you cannot think of coming into Fetters again.

BUT, Cousin, *says the Lady*, I am not so easy as you think I am.

DEAR Madam, *says the Cousin*, what can be more happy? Why, you have nothing to trouble you, and no Body to control you.

WELL, Cousin, *says the Lady*, no more I won't, if I marry; for I am resolved to take a young Man, that has his Dependence upon me, and I am sure to preserve my Authority with him.

O, Madam, *says the Cousin*, pray GOD you don't find your self mistaken.[107]

Words matter throughout, even for a tradesman:

The tradesman need not be offended at my condemning them *as it were* to a plain and homely stile; easy, plain, and familiar language is the beauty of speech in general, and is the excellency of all writing, on whatever subject, or to whatever persons they are we write or speak. The end of speech is that men might understand one another's meaning; certainly, that speech, or that way of speaking which is most easily understood is the best way of speaking. If any man was to ask me, which would be supposed to be a perfect stile, or language, I would answer that in which a man speaking to five hundred people, of all common and various capacities, idiots or lunaticks excepted, should be understood by all in the same manner with one another; and in the same sense which the speaker intended to be understood, this would certainly be a most perfect stile.[108]

And yet, as Michael Seidel comments, 'It is characteristic of Defoe locutions that the very impossibility of describing something suffices for its realistic description'.[109] In *Crusoe* our author declares that, 'I cannot explain by any possible Energy of Words', 'Nothing can describe the confusion of thought', and 'I believe it is impossible to express to the Life what the Extasies and Transport of the Soul are' before precisely doing so. In *The Storm* we are told, 'Horror and Confusion seiz'd upon all, whether on Shore or at Sea: No Pen can describe it, no Tongue can express it, no Thought conceive it, unless some of those who were at the extremity of it', as a preface for two hundred pages of description.

Pragmatic to a point, Defoe was prepared to admit to some variety of approach, especially in the face of the Augustan condescension of Swift, Pope, and the grandees of the old books:

Let not those Gentlemen who are criticks in Stile, in Method or Manner, be angry that I have never pull'd off my Cap to them in humble Excuse for my loose way of treating the World as to Language, Expression, and Politeness of Phrase; Matters of this Nature differ from most things a Man can write. When I am busied writing Essays and Matters of Science, I shall address them for their Aid, and take as much care to avoid their Displeasure as becomes me; but when I am upon the Subject of Trade, and

Variety of Casual Story, I think my self a little loose from the Bonds of Cadence and Perfections of Stile, and satisfie my self to be explicit, easie, free, and very plain; and for all the rest, *Nec Careo, Nec Curo* [I do not miss it nor care about it].[110]

Defoe would write on trade until the end of his life. At the start of *Augusta Triumphans Or, the Way to Make London the Most Flourishing City in The Universe* (1728) he declares,

I have but a short time to live, nor would I waste my remaining thread of life in vain, but having often lamented sundry public abuses, and many schemes having occurred to my fancy . . . I was resolved to commit them to paper before my departure, and leave, at least, a testimony of my good will to my fellow-creatures.[111]

He did not feel the same about the novels, which stopped with *Roxana* in 1724 as abruptly as they had begun with *Crusoe* just five years earlier. Michael Shinagel suggests that *Roxana* stretched its author to his mental and ethical limits:

Defoe no longer was able to control his imagination or his material and being a good Puritan he decided not to tempt the devil any longer. He ceased writing imaginative biographies in which he identified with his creations not wisely but too well.[112]

For *Roxana* this rings more true than, say, *Captain Singleton, Colonel Jack, A Journal of the Plague Year,* or *Memoirs of a Cavalier,* where the principal protagonists are male and the settings more social than intimate. It certainly wasn't the case that Defoe lacked compositional energy, even into his late sixties in an era when that was a very advanced age.

Finis

When he was sixty-five, Defoe made the brave decision to undergo an operation to remove the gallstones that had been afflicting him for years. Spoiler alert: an account follows, please take a deep breath before reading Paula Backscheider's description of a procedure conducted more than a century before the discovery of anaesthesia:

> Defoe would be strapped to the board at his back and his wrists tied to his ankle; the 'three or four strong and courageous Attendants . . . generally necessary . . . to secure the Patient firmly in the proper posture' would hold him down and keep his bent legs apart. The surgeon would insert a long, silver catheter through the opening in the penis so that he could locate the urethra and bladder easily. He would then make a small incision from behind the scrotum towards the anus, cut open the urethra there, and insert a probe, a catheter, and then forceps to remove the stone. In some cases a scoop or even special forceps with teeth to crush large stones had to be used. Throughout the operation, the surgeon pressed the stones forward with fingers inserted in the rectum.[113]

It is perhaps unsurprising that Backscheider believes that it was from this point that Defoe's writing loses its optimism, and, of course, the operation may in and of itself have put a stop to his writing of outright fiction (the third volume of *A Tour thro' the Whole Island of Great Britain* was published the next year and is generally reckoned to contain invented and borrowed passages as well as personal memoir).

As we have seen in *Crusoe*, Defoe already possessed a keen interest in matters metaphysical, and this now takes on a higher profile, *The Political History of the Devil* being published in 1726 and *An Essay on the History and Reality of Apparitions* the following year. Both books certainly contain elements of humour and reassurance, Defoe showing no sign—still less fear—of any impending demise as signalled in *Augusta Triumphans*. Indeed, in *An Essay*, Defoe claims,

> Guilt is only the reason of Fear . . . Fear is a Horror of the Soul, in apprehension of some farther Evil yet out of view; unseen and therefore terrible; merited and therefore terrible. If there were no Guilt in the Mind, Death it self would be no Evil, and therefore not the subject of our Fear; nor is Death it self our Fear now, as it is in itself a meer passing out of life, otherwise as it is an inlet of some terrible state beyond it.

In a similar vein—very much in the style of *Crusoe III*—he seeks to settle the nerves as well as the presumptions of his readers:

Spectre and *Apparition* make a great Noise in the World; and have (at least formerly) had a great Influence among us. Between our Ancestors laying too much stress upon them, and the present Age endeavouring wholly to explode and despise them, the World seems hardly ever to have come to a right Understanding about them. Some despise them in such an extraordinary manner . . . as if nothing but seeing the *Devil* could satisfie them there was such a person . . . Again, some People are so horribly frighted at the very mention of an Apparition, that they cannot go two steps in the dark, or in the dusk of the Evening without looking behind them; and if they see but a Bat fly, they think of the Devil, because of its wings; and as for a Screech Owl, at its first appearance, they make no scruple of running into the House in a Fright, affirming they have seen the Devil.[114]

If he had stopped writing novels, Daniel Defoe had not stopped dealing, or double-dealing as some charged. His last major 'project' involved the purchase and renting out of land outside Colchester, the usual misunderstanding about payments, equity, and credit abounding from the start. There was no strict need for this as Mary's brother Samuel had left her a sizeable legacy (explicitly excluding Daniel from the inheritance). As ever, whilst he could write plenty of words, Defoe was lamentably bad at keeping records of agreements and numbers, with matters ending in court.

In *The Compleat English Tradesman* Defoe had celebrated 'the Capers and Anchovies from *Leghorn*', what are they but Sauces to whet our gorg'd Appetites, and to assist our surfeited Stomachs, overcharg'd with quantities of Food, help our Gluttony, and prompt us to repeat our Cravings, and call for more?

If this seems like a Presbyterian refusal of luxury, Defoe's practice was running contrary to his words. The records of the County Court of London and Middlesex of 1730, the last year of his life, report,

> *Paul Croney*, of Allhallows Barking, was indicted for feloniously stealing a Barrel of Anchovies, the Goods of *Daniel de Foe*, the 6th of February last. *Jacob Neal* depos'd, That he saw the Prisoner bring the Barrel of Anchovies in his Apron from *Brown's* Key, where a great many more lay, to *Galley-Key*, where he apprehended him. The Prisoner pleaded he was hir'd by a Man to carry them, but could not produce the Person; the Fact being plainly prov'd, the Jury found him guilty.[115]

One can barely say that Defoe won this case, but at least he did not lose it.

The last letters we have are from 1729 and 1730 directed to Sophia, his favourite daughter, and her new husband, Henry Baker, with whom Defoe had previously conducted a pretty miserable haggle over Sophia's dowry. They are sad reading. Defoe is depressed and in hiding. He had been sued for a debt in the Court of Chancery by one Mary Brooke, who he did not know but who was pressing a claim dating from the 1690s that had been inherited at least twice in wills. Presumably Defoe and his reputation were now so infamous that even the most tenuous claim to be a creditor stood some chance in court. Defoe counter-sued, but lost and took to flight. Equally, he is most upset that his elder son, Daniel, who was a successful businessman, was not looking after the rest of the family, but it is quite possible that the son had transferred his property precisely to keep it out of Mrs. Brooke's hands.

The letter to Baker of 30 August 1730 from 'About two Miles from Greenwich, Kent' shows flashes of defiance within a deeper despondency:

> I am at this Time under a weight of very heavy Illness, which I think will be a Fever, I take this Occasion to vent my Grief in the Breasts who I know will make prudent use of it, and tell you, that nothing but this has conquered or could conquer me. *Et tu! Brute* . . . Excuse my Infirmity, I can say no more; my Heart is too full. I ask only one Thing of you as a dying request. Stand by them when I am gone, and let them not be wrong'd . . . It adds to my Grief that it is so difficult to me to see you. I am at a distance from London in Kent; nor have I lodging in London, nor have I been at that Place in the Old Bailey, since I wrote you I was removed from it . . . I am so near my Journey's end, and am hastening to the Place where the Weary are at Rest, and where the Wicked cease to trouble . . . Kiss my dear Sophy once more for me; and if I must see her no more, tell her this is from a Father that loved her above all his Comforts, to his last Breath.
>
> Your unhappy
>
> D.F.

In a postscript Defoe mentions the sale of the Stoke Newington house, which Baker would later buy. We don't know if the family ever saw him again, but it is not impossible since Daniel Defoe died, 'of lethargy', on 24 April 1731 in a lodging house in Ropemaker's Alley, a few yards both from St. Giles Cripplegate, where his bust stands alongside those of Cromwell and Milton, and also close to Whitecross Street where Mary had a house.

Mrs. Brooke never got any money out of the family since City of London Custom ensured that the legacy passed to the widow, as Defoe appeared confident it would. Mary died the following year and may have been buried alongside her husband in Bunhill Fields. The original modest headstone was replaced by the seventeen-foot marble pillar that currently stands on a four-foot base, erected in September 1870 after a global fund-raising campaign from children around the world. Like the first memorial, it identifies the plot as the last resting place of the author of *Robinson Crusoe*.

James Sutherland ended his biography of 1937 with a form of words that seems entirely apposite and that cannot really be bettered:

> There have been few men of any generation so indomitably alive for seventy years as Daniel Defoe was alive, and who dying can make us feel so sharply the finality of death. When he breathed his last in the lodging-house in Ropemaker's Alley, a source of energy was suddenly cut off, a window was darkened that had thrown its beams across all England.[116]

*

Obelisk monument to Daniel Defoe, 1870. Photo by Sarah Ainslie.

DANIEL DEFOE

Defoe's original headstone is now on display in the Hackney Museum. Removed by Samuel Horner of Bournemouth, who had built the marble obelisk, it stood in the front garden of 56 Portswood Road, Southampton, until 1945 and was only restored to the author's home street in 1958. The Stoke Newington house was demolished in 1865. There are websites that seek to identify precisely where it and the walled garden stood in terms of the current built environment. A blue plaque is fixed halfway up a brick house on the junction of Defoe Road and Stoke Newington Church Street. The pub opposite, long known as the 'Daniel Defoe' now bears the title of 'The Clarence Tavern' for no obvious reason; it markets itself as a gastro-pub. At the end of the road the old 'Robinson Crusoe' has been rede-nominated 'The Clissold Park Tavern', which sells pizzas. This is a source of some consternation to Ken Garip, founder and owner—'it's my brain-child'—of 'Defoe Tyres', located opposite the blue plaque. He can no longer give instructions on the phone to clients with punctures needing repair in terms of Daniel Defoe and his most famous book. Does he think the pubs might be renamed on the three hundredth anniversary of the publication of *Robinson Crusoe*? 'It's possible'.

Acknowledgments

Matthew Watson reawakened my interest in *Crusoe* when he gave a paper at Queen Mary University of London (QMUL) in March 2011 on the use/abuse of the story in the promotion of neoclassical economics. I can't remember if there were two or three people in the audience, but I recall the paper as if it were yesterday and I have been sensible enough to keep the notes. Thanks, Mat.

More than any other person, Arianna Bove is responsible for this book being written. Arianna and I taught a very popular course on 'Utopias and Dystopias' for several years at QMUL. One week was devoted to the use of *Crusoe* as representative of an 'economic dream-world'. I gave that lecture but Arianna designed most of the course. For me she was an exemplary colleague, and her students plainly loved her and the way she taught. But she was drummed out of her job in the new world of higher education where a lecturer in ethics can be gleefully replaced by two in marketing. Now that she is free to be a scholar on her own terms, expect to hear more from Arianna.

I cannot name everyone else who has been so generous in supporting the composition of this little book or in trying to stem its errors, but there are some who simply have to be mentioned. Fellow London Loopers—Sarah Ainslie, Gregor Claude, Alex Fry, Emma Ridgway, Catherine Townsend, and Penny Woolcock—heard out early vocal versions with ambulant amiability. They all remember the civet cats. Sarah also took the photographs here. Likewise, fellow occupants of the Tiptree Stand at Chelmsford's county cricket ground tolerated mumbled asides on the early 1700s as we watched Essex win the championship and then lose it. Thanks from beyond the boundary to Peter Brett, Rick Saull, David Williams, and Ray Kiely, who also subjected the progress of the manuscript to the friendliest of audits. McNamara and McNamee, rooftop sprites from down-under, kept my inner mind alliteratively focused. I promised Olivia Martinez that I wouldn't grass her up as the source of 'Crusoe on the campus', but now I have—some of Daniel Defoe's defects rub off; sorry, Darling. Carmen Soliz took me to Charleston, and warmly assumed the slack in my study of modern Bolivia caused by the present excursus to different places in earlier times. John King, who knows all these books better than I, lent quiet, brotherly support, as he ever has.

Guy Holmes and Biza Stenfert Kroese, Mary Clare Lennon and Ian Roxborough, shared holiday homes with the generosity that only truly, sensibly, holiday-minded people can do. I thank them with all my heart for prising me away from the desk. Terry Eagleton kindly tutored me in French theory on a picket 'line' in Didcot in the 1970s. Although the world supply of dartboards was not on that occasion choked off, I benefited hugely from his smiling, simile-laden explications of Gallic abstraction. Colin Robinson has been the most patient and understanding editor and friend for many

ACKNOWLEDGMENTS

years. If he had been anything else you wouldn't be reading these lines. He is a Liverpool supporter, but nobody's perfect. Thanks to Colin and his team, especially Amanda Bartlett for editing in such a generous yet precious way.

Closer to home, and the uncertain nervous pulse, I owe a debt of gratitude of Defoe-like dimensions to Barbara, Bill, Caro, Kully, and Penny. Would they accept 15/- in the pound?

It might be that those of us who loved Utako Ikeda are moving on from the sorrow that she is gone to the celebration that she was here. At her funeral we were given seeds to plant for the future, but I am no gardener, so I hope that these words will do instead.

Notes

PREFACE

1. 'Robinson Crusoe', *History Workshop Journal* 10 (1980): 7.
2. Paul K. Alkon, *Defoe and Fictional Time* (Athens, Georgia: 1979), 105.
3. Pat Rogers, *Defoe. The Critical Heritage* (London: 1972), 8.
4. Maximilian E. Novak and Carl Fisher, eds., *Approaches to Teaching Defoe's Robinson Crusoe* (New York: 2005), 16–19.
5. Pat Rogers, *Robinson Crusoe* (London: 1979), 12.
6. Robert H. MacDonald, 'The Creation of the Ordered World in *Robinson Crusoe*', *The Dalhousie Review* (1976): 24.
7. See, for instance, William T. Hastings, 'Errors and Inconsistencies in Defoe's Robinson Crusoe', *Modern Language Notes* 27:6 (June 1912).
8. All quotations below are from the 2001 Penguin edition edited by the great Defoe scholar John Richetti.
9. Marginalia in Coleridge's copy of the 1812 edition, reproduced in Rogers, *Critical Heritage*, 84.
10. *Colonial Encounters: Europe and the Native Caribbean 1492–1797* (London: 1986), 186.
11. E. Mandel, ed., *Capital*, I, (London: 1867/1976), 169–170.; 'Introduction: Friday on the Potomac', in *Race-ing Justice, En-gendering Power: Essays on Anita Hill, Clarence Thomas, and the Construction of Social Reality* (New York: 1992), xxvii, cited in Roxann Wheeler, '"My Savage", "My Man": Racial Multiplicity in "Robinson Crusoe"', *ELH* 62:4 (Winter 1995), 854.
12. Ian Watt, cited in Rogers, *Robinson Crusoe*, 120.
13. James Sutherland, *Defoe* (London: 1937), 89–92, 231.

14. Manuel Schonhorn, *Defoe's Politics: Parliament, Power, Kingship, and Robinson Crusoe* (Cambridge: 1991), 161.

15. P.N. Furbank and W.R. Owens, *The Canonisation of Daniel Defoe* (New Haven: 1988); *Defoe De-Attributions* (London: 1994).

16. Jürgen Habermas, *The Structural Transformation of the Public Sphere* (Cambridge: 1989); Michel Foucault, *Discipline and Punish; The Birth of the Prison* (London: 1975).

17. J.G.A. Pocock, *The Machiavellian Moment. Florentine Political Thought and the Atlantic Republican Tradition* (Princeton: 1975); *Virtue, Commerce, and History* (Cambridge: 1985).

18. 19 April 1709, cited in John Richetti, *The Life of Daniel Defoe* (Oxford: 2005), 86.

19. Cited in Maximillian E. Novak, *Daniel Defoe. Master of Fictions* (Oxford: 2001), 430.

20. *An Appeal to Honour and Justice, Though It Be of His Worst Enemies. Being A True Account of His Conduct in Public Affairs* (London: 1715), 19–20.

21. *An Essay Upon Projects* (London: 1697), 8, 98.

ROBINSON CRUSOE

1. Richetti, *Life of Daniel Defoe*, 213.

2. 'Un-Erasing "Crusoe": "Farther Adventures" in the Nineteenth Century', *Book History* 9 (2006): 114, 100.

3. *Robinson Crusoe. The Farther Adventures of Robinson Crusoe* (London: 1953), 250. Subsequent citations of this work will refer to this edition, by Collins, with page numbers included in the text.

4. S.S. Prawer, *Karl Marx and World Literature* (Oxford: 1976), 336–7.

5. *Dreams of Adventure, Deeds of Empire* (London: 1980), 57, cited in Richetti, *Life of Defoe*, 217.

6. James Kelly, 'Defoe's Library', *The Library* 3:1 (Sept. 2002); Stephen Bertman, 'Defoe and "the Footprints of Man"', *Digital Defoe* 5:1 (Fall 2013); Diana Souhami, *Selkirk's Island* (London: 2001); Tim Severin, *Seeking Robinson Crusoe* (London: 2002).

7. William Dampier, *A New Voyage Round the World. The Journal of an English Buccaneer*, ed. G. Milton (London: 1697/1998), 11.

NOTES

8. *Oroonoko. A True History* (London: 1688/2016), 18; Edward D. Seeber, 'Oroonoko and Crusoe's Man Friday', *Modern Languages Quarterly* 12:3 (1951): 288.

9. Dampier, 53–54.

10. Souhami, 44.

11. Steele's account is reproduced in Rogers, *Robinson Crusoe*, 160–162; Woodes Rogers, *A Cruising Voyage Round the World* (London: 1712/1928), 91–94.

12. Souhami, 101. The basis of this supposition—Selkirk's notching of the ears of the goats he had 'used' was confirmed to the author by an islander as commonplace if not exactly natural.

13. He didn't like maypoles or cosmetics either. Novak, *Daniel Defoe*, 276.

14. Severin, 253 ff., 290–294.

15. Richard Hamblyn, ed., *The Storm* (London: Penguin, 2005).

16. John Campbell, *Lives of the British Admirals*, IV (London: 1817), 237–263.

17. John Robert Moore, 'Defoe and Shakespeare', *Shakespeare Quarterly* 19:1 (Winter 1968): 80.

18. Bertman, 'Defoe and "the Footprints of Man"', 133.

19. David Fausett, *The Strange Surprizing Sources of "Robinson Crusoe"* (Amsterdam: 1994); Ton J. Broos, 'Did Daniel Defoe do Dutch?', *Canadian Journal of Netherlands Studies* 33:1 (2012).

20. The full title was *The Life and Strange Surprizing Adventures of Mr D….. De F…, of London, Hosier, who Has Liv'd above fifty years by himself, in the Kingdoms of* North *and* South Britain. *The various Shapes he has appear'd in, and the Discoveries he has made for the Benefit of his Country. In a DIALOGUE between* Him, Robinson Crusoe, *and his Man* Friday. With REMARKS Serious and Comical upon the life of CRUSOE. All this is presented in Paul Dottin, ed., *Robinson Crusoe Examin'd and Criticis'd* (London: 1923). The quote on Pope is at 33.

21. Quoted in ibid., 30. Curll sponsored Gildon's attack on Pope.

22. *Prose Works*, IV, 7–8, quoted in John Frederic Ross, *Swift and Defoe. A Study in Relationship* (Berkeley: 1941), 13–14.

23. *Prose Works*, III, 13–14, quoted in Richard I. Cook, '"Mr Examiner" and "Mr Review": The Tory Apologetics of Swift and Defoe', *Huntington Library Quarterly* 29:2 (Feb. 1966): 128.

24. *Mere Nature Delineated* (1726), 45, quoted in Ross, 27.

25. For erudite analysis of the epistemological and ontological compass available to readers of Swift, see Warren Montag, *The Unthinkable Swift: The Spontaneous Philosophy of a Church of England Man* (London: 1994); Martin C. Battestin, 'The Critique of Freethinking from Swift to Sterne', *Eighteenth-Century Fiction* 15:3–4 (2003).

26. Ross; Katsumi Hashinuma, 'The Economic Themes in *Gulliver's Travels*', *Hitotsubashi Journal of Arts and Sciences* 42 (2001): 41–58.

27. Michael McKeon, *The Origins of the English Novel, 1600–1740* (London: 1987), 335; Jonathan Swift, *Gulliver's Travels*, ed. Claude Rawson (London: 1726/2005), 276.

28. Jean-Jacques Rousseau, 'Introduction', in *Émile*, ed. P.D. Jimack (London: 1974), viii. *The Social Contract* (Oxford: 1994), 48.

29. Rousseau, 147.

30. Joachim Heinrich Campe, *An Abridgement of the New Robinson Crusoe: An Instructive and Entertaining History, for the Use of Children of Both Sexes* (London: 1789), 24–25. This edition cost 2/6d. It is perhaps a mark of Campe's curiosity and confidence that at the time of the publication in London he was taking the twenty-one-year-old Wilhelm von Humboldt to Paris to witness the French Revolution.

31. Campe, 141.

32. Campe, 183.

33. Rogers, *Crusoe*, 141.

34. T.M. Raysor, ed., *Coleridge's Miscellaneous Criticism* (London: Penguin, 1936), 294. The Penguin edition, like several others, employs a comma rather than a semi-colon, but the sense is not thereby lost. The marginalia appear to date from the 1830s.

35. Quoted in Rogers, *Crusoe*, 142.

36. Wilkie Collins, *The Moonstone* (London: 1868/1999), 8–9.

37. Article in the *Cornhill* Magazine, 1868, reprinted in *Hours in a Library* (1874) and quoted in Rogers, *Crusoe*, 145.

NOTES

38. 'The Humanities on the River Kwai' in *The Literary Imagination. Selected Essays*, ed. Bruce Thompson (Stanford: 2002), 230; Mary MacKay, 'The Wartime Rise of the *Rise of the Novel*', *Representations* 119:1 (Summer 2012).

39. Lennard J. Davis, 'Who Put the *The* in the *Novel*: Identity Politics and Disability in Novel Studies', *Novel* 31 (1998): 80, quoted in Nicholas Seager, *The Rise of the Novel: A Reader's Guide to Essential Criticism* (London: 2012); highly recommended for novices of every age.

40. *Myth in Primitive Psychology* (London: 1926), 18–19, quoted in Watt, '*Robinson Crusoe* as a Myth', *Essays in Criticism* I:2, (April 1951): 96.

41. Watt, '*Crusoe* as Myth', 107.

42. Watt, '*Crusoe* as Myth', 110. 'In the most influential account of this process, Max Weber's *The Protestant Ethic and the Spirit of Capitalism* of 1904, the meticulous Calvinist accounting of time and expenditure, originally tethered to the promise of salvation, was said to provide underpinnings for the abstinent and calculative mentality of early capitalism. That in turn supplied the crucial psychic component at the core of the extraordinary expansion of commercial and industrial capitalism in the eighteenth and nineteenth centuries'. Ira Katznelson and Gareth Stedman Jones, eds., *Religion and the Political Imagination* (Cambridge: 2010), 4.

43. Watt, '*Crusoe* as Myth', 111.

44. Watt, *The Rise of the Novel. Studies in Defoe, Richardson and Fielding* (London: 1957), 35.

45. Watt, *The Rise of the Novel*, 65.

46. Watt, *The Rise of the Novel*, 66.

47. Watt, *The Rise of the Novel*, 73, quoting the 1937 French edition of *Notes on Philosophy and Political Economy*.

48. Watt, *The Rise of the Novel*, 76–77.

49. Ian Watt, 'Serious Reflections on "The Rise of the Novel"', *NOVEL: A Forum on Fiction* i:3 (Spring 1968): 209–210.

50. Ashley Marshall, 'A New Take on the Rise of the Novel', *Huntington Library Quarterly* 73:2 (June 2010): 329.

51. J. Paul Hunter, *Before Novels. The Cultural Contexts of Eighteenth Century English Fiction* (New York: 1990), 66.

52. J. Paul Hunter, *The Reluctant Pilgrim. Defoe's Emblematic Method and the Quest for Form in Robinson Crusoe* (Baltimore: 1966), 19.

53. Hunter, *Reluctant Pilgrim,* 189.

54. Quoted in Hunter, *Reluctant Pilgrim,* 32, 33.

55. Rogers, *Crusoe,* 53. Rogers notes that Starr concentrates on Anglican doctrine, whereas Hunter mines the dissenting sermons more fully, which makes most sense for Defoe. The very influential views of Richard Baxter are well represented in the broader interpretative literature, being positively dominant in the work of Weber and Tawney. That lineage would continue through Watt to Habermas, as we will see.

56. *Mere Nature Delineated* (London: 1726), 263, quoted in Novak, *Defoe,* 660.

57. Morgan Strawn, '"Zealous for Their Own Way of Worship": Defoe, Monarchy and Religious Toleration during the War of the Quadruple Alliance', *Eighteenth-Century Fiction* 25:2 (2012–13): 333.

58. *Capital,* I, 169.

59. 'Crusoe's Secret: Daniel Defoe', in *Crusoe's Secret. The Aesthetics of Dissent* (London: 2005), 99.

60. Paulin, *Crusoe's Secret,* 96. 'Just as the word 'alienation', whether used by Hegel, Marx, or later thinkers, implies an anterior state of spiritual, economic, and cultural harmony, whose actual historical existence I question, so Marx's sense of 'bourgeoisie' implies a whole historical and political theory'. Watt, 'Flat-Footed and Fly-Blown': The Realities of Realism', in *The Literal Imagination,* 78.

61. Watt, '*Crusoe* as Myth', 173.

62. Christopher Flint, 'Orphaning the Family: The Role of Kindship in *Robinson Crusoe*', *ELH* 55:2 (Summer 1988): 390–393; Thomas M. Kavanagh, 'Unraveling Robinson: The Divided Self in Defoe's *Robinson Crusoe, Texas Studies in Literature and Language* 20:3 (1978).

63. Robert Maniquis, 'Teaching *The Pilgrim's Progress* and *Robinson Crusoe*; or, From Filthy Mire to the Glory of Things', in Novak and Fisher, eds., *Approaches to Teaching,* 34.

64. *Conjugal Lewdness,* 61, quoted in Richetti, *Life of Daniel Defoe,* 356.

65. *Colonial Encounters,* 186.

NOTES

66. *The Country and the City*, 32. Williams's central theme here is how 'myth functions as memory'.

67. *Colonial Encounters*, 179, 215.

68. I. A. Bell, 'King Crusoe: Locke's Political Theory in *Robinson Crusoe*', in *English Studies*, I, 1988.

69. *Review* vi (1709), 186, quoted in Earle, 69.

70. *Review* iv (1708), 588, 595, quoted in S. Pincus, 'Addison's Empire: Whig Conceptions of Empire in the Early 18ᵗʰ Century', *Parliamentary History* 31:1 (Oct. 2012): 102, 107.

71. *Review* ix, 89, quoted in Earle, 131. Compare that with Marx's *Poverty of Philosophy* of 1847 (49–50): 'Direct slavery is just as much the pivot of bourgeois industry as machinery, credits, etc. Without slavery you have no cotton; without cotton you have no modern industry. It is slavery that gave the colonies their value; it is the colonies that created world trade, and it is world trade that is the precondition of large-scale industry. Thus slavery is an economic category of the greatest importance'.

72. 'Competing Models of Socially Constructed Economic Man: Differentiating Defoe's Crusoe from the Robinson of Neoclassical Economics', *New Political Economy* 16:5 (2011): 610.

73. 'Crusoe, Friday and the Raced Market frame of Orthodox Economics Textbooks', *New Political Economy* (2017). Amongst the contemporary examples Watson cites are: F. Gottheil, *Principles of Economics* (2013), S. Basov, *Microeconomics with Spreadsheets* (2017); and F. Musgrave and E. Kacapyr, *Barron's How to Prepare for the AP Microeconomics/Macroeconomics Advanced Placement Examinations* (2001).

74. 'Rousseau's Crusoe myth: the unlikely provenance of the neoclassical homo economicus', *Journal of Cultural Economy* 10:1 (2017).

75. 'The production of an economic *Robinson Crusoe*', in U. Grapard and G. Hewitson, eds., *Robinson Crusoe's Economic Man: A Construction and Deconstruction* (London: 2011), 17–18. The distinction between classical and neoclassical economic concerns is outlined by William Kern, 'Robinson Crusoe and the Economists' in the same volume, 65.

76. Watson, 'Crusoe, Friday', 2.

77. Prawer, *Karl Marx and World Literature*, 134.

78. 'Da die politische Ökonomie Robinsonaden liebt, erscheine zuerst Robinson auf seiner Insel. Bescheiden, wie er von Haus aus ist, hat er doch verschiedenartige Bedürfnisse zu befriedigen und muß daher nützliche Arbeiten verschiedner Art verrichten, Werkzeuge machen, Möbel fabrizieren, Lama zähmen, fischen, jagen usw'. Ben Fowkes translates this accurately in the 1976 Penguin English edition; most prior translations substitute 'goats' in loyalty to the original book.

79. *Economic Sophisms* (Paris: 1845/Princeton: 1996), 244–6.

80. 'The Use (and Abuse) of Robinson Crusoe in Neoclassical Economics', *History of Political Economy* 48:1 (2016): 47, 45.

81. *Grundrisse*, ed. Martin Nicolaus (London: 1973), 83; 84.

82. *Capital*, I, 170. There are two further mentions. In Chapter Ten on the working day, Marx refers to one Robinson as 'Man Friday' to a cotton-spinner Eskrigge. In Chapter Twenty-five on the general law of capitalist accumulation he accuses Malthus of plagiarising Defoe and others, having no evidence of his own. *Capital*, I, 401, 766.

83. *Karl Marx and World Literature*, 315, 319.

84. *Intelligence and Democratic Action* (Cambridge, Massachusetts: 1960), 76, quoted by W.S. Kern in Grapard and Hewitson, *Robinson Crusoe's Economic Man*, 69.

85. 'Flat-Footed and Fly-Blown', in *The Literal Imagination*, 84, 86. In case the Barthes passage might be deemed the casualty of translation by Watt, who had to learn German three times in his life but had fluent French, here is the original: 'Le réalisme, ici, ce ne peut donc être la copie des choses, mais la connaissance du langage; l'oeuvre la plus 'réaliste' ne sera pas celle qui 'peint' la réalité, mais qui, se servant de monde comme contenu (ce contenu lui-même est d'ailleurs étranger a sa structure, c'est-à-dire a son être), explorera le plus profondément possible la réalité'.

86. 'The *Nautilus* and the Drunken Boat', in *Mythologies* (London: 1973), 65–6.

87. *A Theory of Literary Production* (London: 1978), 208, 240–1.

88. *A Theory of Literary Production*, 241, 246.

89. *How to Live Together. Novelistic Simulations of Some Everyday Spaces* (New York: 2013), xxii.

NOTES

90. *How to Live Together*, 27. 'In Flaubert's short story, Félicité has her parrot Loulou stuffed. In her dying moments, she imagines it to be the incarnation of the Holy Spirit'. Note 12, 181.

91. *The Beast and the Sovereign*, II (Chicago: 2011), 260.

92. *The Beast and the Sovereign*, 48. For David Simpson, 'Through all of Crusoe's initially terrified meditations on its origins—the devil, savages, his own foot—what is most bizarre, that there is one print when two or more would be expected, is something he reflects on not at all'. *Romanticism and the Question of the Stranger* (Chicago: 2013), 8. For a useful review of the original French edition, see David Farrell King, *Research in Phenomenology* 42:3 (2012): 437–466.

93. *The Beast and the Sovereign*, 261, 278.

94. Gilles Deleuze, 'Michel Tournier and the World Without Others', in *Logic of Sense* (London: 2015), 320, cited in *The Beast and the Sovereign*, 27.

95. *Logic of Sense*, 312.

96. *Friday or the Other Island* (London: 1974), 180.

97. Millicent Lenz, 'The Experience of Time and the Concept of Happiness in Michel Tournier's *Friday and Robinson: Life on Speranza Island*', *Children's Literature Association Quarterly* 11:1 (1986): 25.

98. *Friday*, 35; Susan Petit, '"Sexualité Alimentaire et Elémentaire": Michel Tournier's Answer to Freud', *Mosaic* 24:3–4 (1991): 163–177.

99. *Friday*, 97.

100. Lecture, 1911, in Trieste, quoted in Richetti, *Life of Daniel Defoe*, 185.

101. 'Robinson Crusoe', in the *Second Common Reader* (New York: 1932), 48–49.

102. 'Crusoe's Island', in *Collected Poems, 1948–1984* (London: 1986), 69.

103. https://www.poetryfoundation.org/poems/48287/crusoe-in-england.

104. Martin Green, *The Robinson Crusoe Story* (University Park: 1990).

105. J.M. Coetzee, *Foe* (London: 1986), 50.

106. https://www.nobelprize.org/prizes/literature/2003/coetzee/25261-j-m-coetzee-nobel-lecture-2003/.

107. 'Daniel Defoe, *Roxana*', in *Late Essays, 2006–2017* (London: 2017), 2–3, 10–11.

108. *Crusoe's Daughter* (London: 1985), 85–86.

109. *Crusoe's Daughter*, 132.

110. *Crusoe's Daughter*, 220–221.

DANIEL DEFOE

1. Julian Hoppit, *A Land of Liberty? England 1689–1727* (Oxford: 2000), 52, 220.

2. *The Diary of John Evelyn* (Oxford: 1985), 210–211.

3. Quoted in Novak, *Daniel Defoe*, 64.

4. Quoted in Novak, *Daniel Defoe*, 44.

5. David Wootton, ed., *John Locke: Political Writings* (London: 1993), 186.

6. Sutherland, *Defoe*, 23.

7. Hoppit, *A Land of Liberty?* 355.

8. *Review* (31 May 1705), Quoted in Brian Cowan, 'Daniel Defoe's *Review* and the Transformations of the English Periodical', *Huntington Library Quarterly* 77:1 (2014): 98.

9. Novak, *Daniel Defoe*, 38.

10. Novak, *Daniel Defoe*, 84.

11. 'The Bloody Assizes: Whig Martyrdom and Memory after the Glorious Revolution', *Albion* 27 (Fall 1995): 382–3.

12. E.P. Thompson, ed., *Albion's Fatal Tree: Crime and Society in Eighteenth-Century England* (London: 1975); Carl Wennerlind, 'The Death Penalty as Monetary Policy: The Practice and Punishment of Monetary Crime, 1690–1830', *History of Political Economy* 36:1 (2004): 147.

13. Novak, *Daniel Defoe*, 56.

14. Backscheider, *Daniel Defoe*, 56.

15. *An Essay Upon Projects* (London: 1697), 9.

16. *The Compleat English Tradesman*, I (London: 1725), 70, quoted in Novak, *Daniel Defoe*, 102.

17. *The Compleat English Tradesman*, II, (London: 1727), 91.

18. *The Compleat English Tradesman*, II, 205.

NOTES

19. *Review* (10 Jan. 1706), quoted in Sandra Sherman, 'Lady Credit No Lady; or, The Case of Defoe's "Coy Mistress," Truly Stated', *Texas Studies in Literature and Language* 37:2 (1995): 187.

20. *The Compleat English Tradesman*, I, 232, quoted in Sherman, 'Promises, Promises: Credit as Contested Metaphor in Early Capitalist Discourse', *Modern Philology* 94:3 (1997): 341.

21. J.G.A. Pocock, *Virtue, Commerce and History* (Cambridge: 1985), 48, 103.

22. J.G.A. Pocock, *The Machiavellian Moment* (Princeton: 1975), 446–7.

23. *Review* (20 Jan. 1708, 24 Jan. 1708), quoted in Steve Pincus, 'Addison's Empire: Whig Conceptions of Empire in the Early Eighteenth Century', *Parliamentary History* 31:1 (2012) 102, 107.

24. Pocock, *Virtue, Commerce and History*, 231.

25. *An Essay Upon Projects*, 5.

26. *An Essay Upon Projects*, 73.

27. Quoted in Sutherland, *Defoe*, 56.

28. Hoppit, *A Land of Liberty?* 239.

29. Quoted in L.S. Horsley, 'Rogues or Honest Gentlemen: The Public Characters of Queen Anne Journalists', *Texas Studies in Literature and Language* 18:2 (1976): 206.

30. Hoppit, *A Land of Liberty?* 33.

31. Hoppit, *A Land of Liberty?* 30.

32. Hoppit, *A Land of Liberty?* 126; Wennerlind, 'Death Penalty', 134.

33. Earle, *World of Defoe*, 155.

34. Hoppit, *A Land of Liberty?* 129

35. James T. Boulton, ed., *Selected Writings of Daniel Defoe* (Cambridge: 1965), 36, 50.

36. Quoted in J.A. Downie *To Settle the Succession of the State. Literature and Politics, 1678–1750* (London: 1994), 51–2.

37. *Selected Writings*, 52–85.

38. Quoted in J. P. Kenyon, *Revolution Principles. The Politics of Party 1689–172* (Cambridge: 1977), 58–9.

39. Quoted in Kenyon, *Revolution Principles*, 91.

40. Quoted in Richetti, *Daniel Defoe*, 41.

41. Backscheider, *Daniel Defoe*, 65.

42. Geoffrey Holmes, *The Trial of Dr Sacheverell* (London: 1973), 17.

43. Holmes, *The Trial of Dr Sacheverell*, 17, 63.

44. *Selected Writings*, 88, 94, 95, 96, 99.

45. Quoted in Novak, *Daniel Defoe*, 179.

46. Quoted in Backscheider, *Daniel Defoe*, 104.

47. *Selected Writings*, 86.

48. G.H. Healey, ed., *The Letters of Daniel Defoe* (Oxford: 1955), 1–3.

49. Backscheider, *Daniel Defoe,* 108–115, provides the most detailed account of the trial and punishment.

50. *Selected Writings*, 101, 103, 106.

51. Quoted in Novak, *Daniel Defoe*, 191.

52. *An Essay Upon Projects*, 13.

53. Backscheider, *Daniel Defoe*, 123.

54. 'The Public Sphere', *New German Critique* 3 (1974), 49, quoted in Geoff Eley, 'Nations, Publics and Political Cultures', in Craig Calhoun, ed., *Habermas and the Public Sphere* (Cambridge, Massachusetts: 1992), 289.

55. H.G. Gadamer, *Truth and Method* (New York: 1975), 513–4, quoted in Habermas, *The Structural Transformation of the Public Sphere* (Cambridge: 1989), 252.

56. Habermas, in fact, suggests far higher levels of illiteracy than those given by Hoppit, *A Land of Liberty?* 169.

57. *Structural Tranformation*, 59.

58. Calhoun, *Habermas and the Public Sphere*, 9; Benedict Anderson, *Imagined Communities. Reflections on the Origins and Spread of Nationalism* (London: 1983).

59. 'An introduction to the coffee-house: A discursive model', *Language and Communication* 28 (2008): 156. Ellis qualifies Habermas's model by noting that the coffeehouse introduced new, less tangible hierarchies and was really only congenial to its regular customers.

60. J.A. Downie 'How useful to eighteenth-century English studies is the paradigm of the "bourgeois public sphere"?', *Literature Compass* 1 (2003): 2; Mark Knights, 'History and Literature in the Age of Defoe and Swift', *History Compass* 3 (2005): 2. Methodological

transgressions can occur even within analytical 'families'. When, two years after Habermas published his book, Perry Anderson suggested in a head-clearing piece that, 'England had the first, most mediated and least pure bourgeois revolution of any major European country', Edward Thompson bestrode his rhetorical high horse much more noisily than did Ian Watt: 'I am objecting to a model which concentrates attention upon one dramatic episode—*the* Revolution—to which all that goes before and after must be related; and which insists upon an ideal type of this Revolution against which all others may be judged. Minds which thirst for a tidy Platonism very soon become impatient with actual history. The French Revolution was a fundamental moment in the history of the West . . . But because it was a gigantic experience it was not necessarily a typical one'. Perry Anderson, 'Origins of the Present Crisis', *New Left Review* 23 (1964), reprinted in *English Questions* (London: 1992); E.P. Thompson, 'The Peculiarities of the English', *Socialist Register* 2 (1965), reprinted in *The Poverty of Theory*, London 1978, 47.

61. Knights, 'History and Literature', 6.

62. E.P. Thompson, 'Eighteenth-century English society: Class struggle without class?', *Social History* 3:2 (1978): 141, 143–4. The thrust of the argument here, of course, is not so different to that made by Anderson; Thompson was piqued by what he thought was a presumptuous style.

63. Richard Hamblyn, ed., *The Storm* (London: 1704/2005), 57.

64. Quoted in Introduction, *The Storm*, xxiii.

65. *The Storm*, 4.

66. *The Storm*, 7.

67. *The Storm*, 11.

68. *The Storm*, 15.

69. Quoted in Novak, *Daniel Defoe*, 278. L'Estrange, 'the Bloodhound of the Press', was the main Stuart enforcer of censorship.

70. Backscheider, *Daniel Defoe*, 171.

71. Quoted in Sutherland, *Defoe*, 122.

72. *Letters*, 97–8, 100, 101–2.

73. Quoted in D.W. Hayton, ed., 'Introduction, Daniel Defoe', in *The History of the Union of Great Britain, Part 1* (London: 1709/2002), 3.

74. Hoppit, *A Land of Liberty?* 250–3.

75. David Macree, 'Daniel Defoe, the Church of Scotland, and the Union of 1707', *Eighteenth-Century Studies* 7:1 (1973): 68.

76. *Letters*, 355.

77. *Letters*, 127.

78. J.A. Downie, 'Secret Service Payments to Daniel Defoe, 1710–1714', *The Review of English Studies* 30 (Nov. 1979): 437.

79. *Letters*, 132.

80. *Letters*, 141.

81. *Letters*, 146.

82. *Letters*, 158–9.

83. *Letters*, 211.

84. *Letters*, 235.

85. Daniel Defoe, *An Appeal to Honour and Justice, Though It Be of His Worst Enemies* (London: 1715), 15.

86. Paula Backscheider, 'John Russell to Daniel Defoe: Fifteen Unpublished Letters from Scotland', *Philological Quarterly* 61:2 (1982).

87. Quoted in J.A. Downie, 'Daniel Defoe and the General Election of 1708 in Scotland', *Eighteenth-Century Studies* 8:3 (1975): 324. For a modern scholarly appraisal of the political management of the Union, see the work of Karin Bowie, particularly 'Public Opinion, Popular Politics and the Union of 1707', *The Scottish Historical Review* 82:2 (2003).

88. *Appeal*, quoted in Novak, *Daniel Defoe*, 363.

89. W.A. Speck, 'The Current State of Sacheverell Scholarship', *Parliamentary History* (2012), 20.

90. Quoted in Sutherland, *Defoe*, 171–2.

91. Quoted in Novak, *Daniel Defoe*, 353.

92. Geoffrey Holmes, 'The Sacheverell Riots: The Crowd and the Church in early Eighteenth-Century England', *Past and Present* 72 (1976).

93. Quoted in P. K. Monod, *Jacobitism and the English People, 1688–1788* (Cambridge: 1993), 177–8.

NOTES

94. *Letters,* 270–1.

95. 'The Conduct of the Allies and of the Late Ministry in Beginning and Carrying on the Present War', in A. Rose and D. Wooley, eds., *Jonathan Swift: Major Works* (Oxford: 2003), 651–2.

96. 'English Projects and Ventures in the South Seas, 1670–1750', in John Flint and Glyndwr Williams, eds., *Perspectives of Empire* (New York: 1973), 37.

97. Quoted in *Perspectives of Empire,* 37.

98. *Review* (12 July 1711), quoted in *Perspectives of Empire,* 40.

99. *Letters,* 346–7.

100. *An Essay on the South-Sea Trade* (London: 1712), 37–8, quoted in *Perspectives on Empire,* 42.

101. *Mist's Journal* (30 April 1720), quoted in *Great Bubbles. South Sea Bubble* (London: 2000), 119.

102. *Review* (14 March 1713), quoted in Lawrence Poston, 'Defoe and the Peace Campaign, 1710–1713: A Reconsideration', *Huntington Library Quarterly* 27:1 (1963): 17.

103. William Pittis, *Considerations on the History of the Mitre and Purse* (London: 1714), 2–3, quoted in Novak, *Daniel Defoe,* 467.

104. Quoted in Novak, *Daniel Defoe,* 466–7.

105. *Selected Writings,* 198

106. *Life of Daniel Defoe,* 160.

107. *Conjugal Lewdness,* 232–3.

108. *Selected Writings,* 227.

109. Seidel, *Robinson Crusoe,* 111.

110. *Review,* quoted in Richetti, *Life of Daniel Defoe,* 96.

111. *Augusta Triumphans,* 3–4.

112. *Daniel Defoe and Middle-Class Gentility* (Harvard, 1968), 194, quoted in Earle, *The World of Defoe,* 32.

113. *Daniel Defoe,* 493–5.

114. *An Essay on Apparitions,* 191; Preface.

115. Quoted in G.A. Starr, '"Sauces to whet our gorg'd Appetites": Defoe at Seventy in the Anchovy Trade', *Philological Quarterly* 54 (1975): 533.